TONY DORSETT

Tony "T.D." Dorsett is one of football's most exciting runners. His story is an appealing one—escaping from a small Pennsylvania mill town to become Rookie of the Year with the Dallas Cowboys. The author, a Pennsylvanian herself, has interviewed Tony's coaches and friends from his high school and college years. She tells of the determined effort of a shy, insecure boy to develop his football prowess, an effort so successful it has made him a national sports hero.

Photo courtesy Sports Information Office, University of Pittsburgh

TONY DORSETT

BY
MARCIA McKENNA BIDDLE

JULIAN MESSNER   NEW YORK

Copyright © 1980 by Marcia Biddle

All rights reserved including the right of
reproduction in whole or in part in any form.
Published by Julian Messner, a Simon & Schuster
Division of Gulf & Western Corporation,
Simon & Schuster Building,
1230 Avenue of the Americas,
New York, New York 10020.
JULIAN MESSNER and colophon are trademarks of
Simon & Schuster, registered in the U.S. Patent
and Trademark Office.

Manufactured in the United States of America.

Design by Irving Perkins

Second Printing, 1981

Library of Congress Cataloging in Publication Data

ISBN 0-671-34040-9

Library of Congress Cataloging in Publication Data

Biddle, Marcia McKenna, 1931–
    Tony Dorsett.

    SUMMARY: Presents a biography of the scrappy
running back who was named the NFC "Rookie of the Year"
in 1978.
    1. Dorsett, Tony—Juvenile literature.   2. Football
players—United States—Biography—Juvenile literature.
3. Dallas Cowboys—Juvenile literature.   [1. Dorsett,
Tony.   2. Football players.   3. Afro-Americans—
Biography]   I. Title.
GV939.D67B53   796.332′092′4 [B] [92]   80-18302
ISBN 0-671-34040-9

TONY DORSETT

It was the first day of summer football camp. The Hopewell High Vikings were starting the 1970 season, and the upperclassmen were looking good.

But Head Coach Butch Ross was watching a new sophomore player, who looked like his running speed might blow the numbers off the timer's stopwatch.

"Dorsett's too small," said a coach. "He only weighed in at 140 pounds."

"But he runs like lightning!" Coach Ross said.

The Viking coaches all knew that Tony Dorsett was a fast runner. His speed didn't surprise them, because they knew his brothers. In fact, everybody around the steel mill town of Aliquippa, Pennsylvania, knew that the older Dorsett boys had been among the fastest runners and best football players around.

Ernest and Keith Dorsett had been star runners at Hopewell Area High School. They wore number 33, and so did Tyrone Dorsett, who had made so many touchdowns for the Vikings that everybody started calling him by his initials, which also stood for touchdown. Melvin, the oldest Dorsett brother, was a track star, and another fast runner.

Last year, the Viking coaches had asked Tony about the Dorsett family speed. Before he went into ninth grade, Tony was chosen to go to the high school summer camp as a "cook's helper." Since he was still in junior high, he wasn't allowed to practice yet with the high school team, but the coaches liked to take a few of the good younger boys along to show them what camp was all about.

"And Tony's going to be good," said Ed Kanitra, his junior high coach. He said Tony was a good, fast defensive player in eighth grade, even if he didn't weigh much over a hundred pounds when he started.

One night at that first camp the coaches were talking about some of the good football players who had come from Hopewell. The first name mentioned was Dorsett.

"How did you all get so fast?" the coaches kidded Tony.

Tony laughed. "You'd know if you saw my dad," he said. "When he'd get mad at us, he'd take a switch and start chasing us. You had to be fast, because he was so fast. We had to try to outrun him! You ask any of my brothers—my dad was *fast!*"

Everybody laughed over the idea of all the Dorsett boys trying to run faster than their dad and his switch. Whether or not that was how they got their speed, Coach Ross was glad to know he had another Dorsett coming along. "It's always a luxury to have a Dorsett on the team," Mr. Ross said.

Later that year, the laughing in the Dorsett family stopped for a long time. Tony's brother Melvin died of a heart disease. His death hit Tony hard. It made him grow up a lot, become more serious about everything. He especially wanted to do something for his mother. He wanted to make her proud of him, and happy again.

When he went back to football camp in tenth grade, he was ready to work hard to make the team. Tony had always liked football—with his brothers starring at Hopewell, Tony went to all the high school games with his mom and dad, his sister Juanita, and his little sister Sheree. At home, he heard football at breakfast, dinner, and supper. He learned more about football around his mom's kitchen table than most people ever know.

But Tony hadn't always worked very hard at football in the past. For that reason, his family wasn't sure he'd ever be the player his brothers were. His brothers sometimes yelled at him, "You have to work harder, or you're going to be the sorriest Dorsett of all!"

Myrtle Dorsett, Tony's mother, was more gentle about it. Once, she had watched him straggle off the field after a midget league game. "Son, we'll never have to worry about you playing football much," she smiled. "You're just too slow!"

"I'll show you, Mom," Tony had said. Now he wanted to prove himself. He didn't have to think twice about going out for the team. Football was in the air around Aliquippa. If people weren't playing it, they were talking about it. And Tony knew he had a long family tradition to live up to.

The coaches watched Tony closely. They saw that his thin legs were a lot stronger than they looked. Tony did have strong legs, and so did most of the boys he knew, partly because they were always running up and down hills.

In Hopewell Township, and Aliquippa, where Tony was born on April 7, 1954, people lived in three places—on top of a hill, in the middle of a hill, or at the bottom of a hill. It was hard to find a place to run very far without either going up a hill or down one.

The Dorsetts lived on Mt. Vernon drive, on top of a hill. Because of the hills, and circling boundary lines, the kids who lived in the first house on Mt. Vernon Drive went to school in town, to Aliquippa High, but the ones who lived in the other houses were in Hopewell Township and went to Hopewell High, which was out on another hill.

Butch Ross was in his second year as head coach at Hopewell. He had coached Keith in his senior year and liked him, and now he was impressed with the way Tony was working. He decided to try him at linebacker. He thought Tony was so fast he'd be hard to block, and he was also fast enough to go out in the flat and cover a pass.

He didn't try Tony on offense, because he already had Bill Federoff, an outstanding runner, at tailback. Besides, the coaches said, "In our league, a 140-pound kid can't play both offense and defense. It would be too much punishment."

That league was the Midwestern Athletic Conference (MAC) and it was one of the toughest in all of western Pennsylvania. The newspapers called the MAC teams "Murderers' Row," and every one of their games was like a small war. MAC play was so intense that one school dropped out of the conference, saying that nobody could take that much pressure every week. But the other schools took pride in standing up to that pressure, and boys from the conference were starring on college and pro teams all over the country. Joe Namath was one of them.

Throwing a skinny kid like Tony into a game in that league seemed like throwing him to the sharks. But as the coaches watched him practice they not only liked his speed, they liked his toughness. As small as he was, he could tackle bigger boys, and he could bring them down. "Tony likes to play, and he plays hard and tough,'" Coach Ross said. He made Tony first string linebacker!

Making the team was a big help to Tony in another way, too. It made him feel more at home when he went to class in the big, sprawling modern high school building for the first time. Hopewell High had fifteen hundred students, and only about twenty of them were black. They came to school on one bus, and they could have felt lonely, or different.

Through football, Tony already knew the players and coaches, so he knew he had friends there. Tony had always

Tony never liked to sit on the bench. He looks sad on the sideline, against Ellwood City his junior year. (*Photo courtesy Richard "Butch" Ross*)

been so shy it was hard for him to make new friends. He had been the kind of small boy who ran to stand behind his mother if strangers came around. Peeking around her, he'd watch everything with his big, wide-set eyes, but he wouldn't talk. As a baby, his eyes were so big, so wide-awake and watchful, that Westley Dorsett, his dad, started calling him "Hawkeye."

Hawkeye didn't like to talk very much yet, especially if he didn't know people very well. But Hopewell was a friendly school, and Tony and the other kids felt welcome there. Teachers smiled at them in the hall whether they knew them or not, and they'd stop to help anybody who looked lost.

Getting lost was easy. The halls circled around a center

courtyard, and trying to find the right room was like following a maze in a puzzle book. For the first few days, Tony and all the new students felt lost in the maze most of the time.

John Waters, the principal, was a good friend to all the students, and he liked to kid Tony.

"Hi, Ugly," he'd greet him.

That always made Tony laugh. "I may be ugly, but I'm not *old!*" he'd answer.

If Tony and his friend Ed Wilamowski saw Mr. Waters walking down the hall carrying a pile of books, they would rush over and help him. "These old folks shouldn't be carrying such heavy loads," they'd grin.

Mr. Waters knew Tony was shy, but he thought he could be a leader, too. He found out Tony could get things done. "If I need two hundred chairs moved to the auditorium, all I need to do is let Tony and Ed know about it, and it's done," he said.

Mr. Waters thought Tony was one of the nicest, most polite boys in school. In fact, Tony's whole sophomore class was going to be an outstanding one, he thought.

In several ways, Tony knew he was lucky to be at Hopewell. If he had lived up the street in the first house on Mt. Vernon Drive, he would have gone to Aliquippa High. They had had some racial troubles there in the past few years. Being at Hopewell, Tony missed out on the hassling that he might have run into at the other school.

Besides, Aliquippa's football program had been going downhill for several years. This year, they had only nineteen boys out for the team. They had trouble finding coaches for their junior high team, too, so Tony wouldn't have had the good early training there he did at Hopewell Junior High.

But if Aliquippa's football record wasn't good, Hopewell's wasn't much better. The Hopewell Vikings had won

TONY DORSETT

only three games last year, and lost seven. Coach Ross was hoping for better things this year, but the season turned out to be disappointing. The Vikings ended the season 3-and-7 again. Most of the losses were heartbreakers, by six points or less, though, and the Vikings would have twenty lettermen coming back next year.

One of them was Tony Dorsett. At linebacker, he was second on the team in tackles. Coach Ross liked the way Tony always seemed to be where the football was. He said Tony had a nose for the ball.

Tony was looking forward to next year, but meanwhile basketball season was coming up, and Tony went out for the team. With his speed, he was soon the sixth man on the squad. That was good for a sophomore, especially when Hopewell had a championship team.

In a big game against Beaver, just down the road from Aliquippa, the Vikings were fighting to get into the play-offs. The rivalry between the two schools was always fierce, and during the game it got out of hand.

All through the game, the Beaver team was throwing insults at the Hopewell boys. Tony heard something they said to one of his close friends, a gentle, slow-speaking boy. It was a remark Tony wouldn't stand for. He turned around and hit the boy who had made it. A fight started. It was quickly broken up, but the damage was done.

Tony knew he was in real trouble. His case was sent to the Western Pennsylvania Interscholastic Athletic League (WPIAL), which is the governing body of sports in that part of the state.

The WPIAL suspended Tony. He would not be allowed to participate in any sports again!

CHAPTER II

Tony thought his life was ruined.

But Hopewell stood behind him. Mr. Waters and the coaches wrote letters to the WPIAL asking that Tony be allowed to play again. They said he hadn't been in any other fights, was only defending another player, and had been on good behavior ever since.

The letters did their job. By summer, the WPIAL declared Tony eligible to play again. How happy he was!

His football coaches were happy, too. They thought Tony was a good boy and the punishment had been too harsh. Besides, they had another big problem on their hands—Bill Federoff had graduated. "How are we going to beat Ambridge without a running back?" they were asking each other.

In their summer meetings, the coaches went over their lists very carefully. They were trying to figure out who could run the ball.

One name kept coming up—Tony Dorsett. But Tony had always played defense; he had never carried the ball. The coaches wished they had a runner with a little experience.

Tony did one thing that helped them make up their minds—he started growing. At camp in August, he was up to 150 pounds. That was still not big enough, but the coaches knew after last year how fast and tough he could play. They thought he seemed more mature now, too, and stronger.

"Well," they said, "let's give Tony a try at tailback!"

In a movie of Tony's life, those words would be followed by drum rolls, trumpets, and flashing lights. But at the time the decision didn't seem any more important than the many other decisions the coaches had to make.

Tony was excited about it, but he didn't say much. Of course, he never did say much. He did want to prove himself, though. After his trouble with the WPIAL he wanted to show everybody he was not a troublemaker and was a good football player, too. He did everything the coaches asked him, and he even stayed after practice to run some more.

Tony wanted to do well and make his family proud of him, especially his mom. Tony didn't mind telling people later that he'd always been a "mama's boy." His mom was fun to be with, and she and her youngest son were very close.

A strong woman of great religious faith, Mrs. Dorsett marched the whole family out to church every Sunday and taught the children to depend on "the good Lord" to help them. She taught them to have pride in themselves and their family, and that it was their duty to use their talents to make something of themselves.

To please her, Tony wanted to use his talents. But he didn't know what they were! The only thing he knew was that someday, when he was older, he wanted to buy his mother a big new house. It would be out in the country, away from the steel mill.

The steel mill was part of Aliquippa, the way an engine is part of a locomotive. It was the reason the town was built. The mill stretches for miles along the Ohio River,

The Viking coaches. Front row: Butch Ross and Mike Zaccari. Back: Ed Kanitra, Gene Yanessa, Ralph Veights. (*Photo courtesy Richard "Butch" Ross*)

about twenty miles west of Pittsburgh in the section of western Pennsylvania called the Beaver Valley.

When Westley and Myrtle Dorsett moved to Aliquippa from North Carolina in the early 1940's, she had to spend most of her time scrubbing black soot off everything in the house. The soot drifted through the air from the mill. It was so thick that anything left out on the porch at night would be covered with the black dirt by morning.

Anti-pollution laws forced the mill to stop sending soot from its big stacks even before Tony was born, so the town wasn't as dirty-looking as it once was. Any pollution now was the kind you could breathe and take into your lungs without knowing it.

Westley Dorsett worked in the mill, the Jones and Laughlin Aliquippa works, and belonged to the United Steelworkers of America. For many years, the union had fought for higher wages and better safety conditions in the mills. Now the steelworkers were paid well, but their jobs were still often dirty and sometimes dangerous. To keep from burning their skin, the men who worked near the big furnaces had to wear long, heavy underwear even in the summer.

Tony often saw his dad come home from work worn out and covered with dirt and ashes. "Don't go into the mill," his dad always told him. "You want to get out and do something better."

Tony heard that many times, and when he was very young he promised his mom and dad that someday he would make a name for himself and the family. He would make a lot of money and do something big for them, like getting them that house in the country he dreamed about.

The homes on Mt. Vernon Drive were built as a housing project for black families. There were several buildings in it, with four or five families in each building. They had well-kept yards and there was plenty of room for kids to run. It was a pleasant neighborhood, but it was still a project. Tony wanted something better for his mom.

When he went downtown in Aliquippa, he knew that wasn't the answer for him. Aliquippa's one main street, Franklin Avenue, leads straight to one place—the steel mill. Along Franklin Avenue are boarded-up store fronts where businesses have moved out of town. Houses built by the steel company cling to the tops of the steep hills on both sides of the street. Aliquippa High School's football stadium seems to hang over the street, halfway up a cliff.

Hopewell Township, where Tony lived just outside the Aliquippa borough line, is called, "A friendly place to live." It is a mixture of nationalities; many people are the children and grandchildren of immigrants who came to work in the big mill in the early 1900's. Sports was a big thing that drew the people together. A good football player was always looked up to. One boy who was not an athlete complained, "If you don't play football in Aliquippa, you're nothing."

Since he was a Dorsett, everybody in Hopewell thought Tony would be a good football player. But they wondered whether he'd be as good as his brothers. Even his coaches didn't know yet. In two pre-season games with other schools, the coaches thought Tony showed promise. The local newspaper, the *Beaver County Times*, just called him "a hard-working junior."

How good would he be? Nobody would know that until he was tested in a game. And the biggest test was coming up first: Ambridge.

Ambridge, another steel town a few miles up the river from Aliquippa, had beaten the Vikings last year and won the Beaver County championship. They were favorites to take the MAC championship this year. It was tough to be facing them in the first game.

TONY DORSETT

Coach Ross prepared the team carefully. He was using the I-formation, with Tony setting up behind the fullback, Paul King, in line behind quarterback Alkey Hummell. On defense, Tony was playing the roving, or "monster," back, because Ross knew he was fast enough to come up to the line of scrimmage to make a tackle, drop back to cover a pass, or cover the field from sideline to sideline.

At Ambridge Area High School Stadium, 7,500 people showed up to see the battle. Some of them—the Hopewell Viking fans—were in for a treat. On the first play, Hummell dropped back and threw a short pass to Tony. He caught it, a yard behind an Ambridge defender. He turned on the speed and just outran the tackle. He outran everybody else on the field, too. Tony scored his first touchdown!

The fans screamed and the coaches looked at each other, first in shock, and then with a new gleam in their eyes. Tony looked over at his parents and grinned while his teammates thumped him on the back. He'd been nervous, starting his first game at tailback. He wanted to live up to the number he was wearing—the Dorsett 33.

Now he wasn't nervous. He was feeling great, but he didn't have time to stand around and think about it. The defense had to go in and hold Ambridge.

And they did it. Toward the end of the last quarter, the score was 21–6, Vikings. Tony took the ball on his own 25-yard line. He found a hole on the left side and raced through. Wow! He was running fast!

The fans jumped up. They could hardly believe their eyes. Tony picked up more speed—faster, faster. Tacklers scattered right and left, behind him. Down the field he went, all the way—75 yards for a touchdown!

What a celebration there was! Headlines in Monday's paper said, "Vikes Surprise Easy Winners!"

But Tony was the one who had surprised everybody, in-

Tony outruns a tackler, but the mud is getting deep. (*Photo courtesy Richard "Butch" Ross*)

cluding his coaches. Watching that last run—"*That's* when we realized how much speed and ability he had," they said. For the next games, they decided not to change their strategy, but they wanted to use plays which would get the ball to Tony more than they had planned at first.

The coaches were worried about the next game. West Mifflin North had a weaker team than Ambridge; maybe the Vikings would have a letdown after that big game. And maybe Tony wouldn't have the same kind of game, either. Maybe he wouldn't be able to play like that two weeks in a row.

Could he? In the third quarter against West Mifflin, Tony took a handoff for an off-tackle play. Everything in front of him was blocked. Tony didn't even slow down. He speeded up, accelerated, and ran around the end. He outran the secondary, and went 37 yards to score! The Vikings won 35–6.

Now everybody knew there was another star called "TD" in town. And Hawkeye was shortened to Hawk. In the West Mifflin game, the Hawk ran for 103 yards, scored three TD's, and caught a pass for 23 yards!

Coach Ross now knew what Tony could do. He could take a simple off-tackle play and make it exciting. He could make cuts and spins that Ross had never seen anybody else do.

Hopewell fans flocked to the next game to see the latest Dorsett and newest TD run through the Ellwood City Wolverines. They saw that, but only for a short time.

After Tony threaded his way through the whole Wolverine team for a 16-yard touchdown to make it 12–0 after only five minutes of play in the first quarter, the first team was taken out. They watched while the subs finished the job, winning 48–6.

Sportswriter Ed Rose said in the *Beaver County Times*,

TONY DORSETT

"The Ellwood City Wolverines made one fatal mistake against the Hopewell Vikings—they showed up. The powerful, talent-laden Vikings completely outclassed them."

Hey, maybe the Vikings were unbeatable!

CHAPTER III

The Vikings were going to win the WPIAL championship this year. Everybody was saying so. But Coach Ross
was afraid of that kind of talk. "Tougher games are coming
up," he told the players.

To get to the WPIAL playoffs, the Vikings would have
to go undefeated. If they did that, they would have playoff
games with undefeated teams from other AA conferences.
(The AA rating was based on the number of students in
the school.)

Butler High School was supposed to be the Vikings' next
roadblock. But when the Vikings took only four plays to
score their first touchdown, Butler didn't even look like
a detour. The Vikings didn't put on any long drives, they
just scored long touchdowns.

One was a 60-yard pass interception return by end Joe
Smith. Another was the kind of run that was starting to
make Tony "Hawk" Dorsett famous around the Beaver
Valley. Tony was back to catch a punt, and called for a fair
catch at the 13-yard line. The Butler team didn't like that.
It meant they couldn't tackle him.

"Hey, Hawk—are you a chicken?" they yelled at him.
"Chicken Hawk!"

On the next play, Tony took the ball. He left one tackler

rocking behind him, as if he'd been caught in the wake of a motor boat. He crossed midfield and faked out another. At the 25, he picked up a blocker and shot across the goal line. When he trotted back to the bench, he was laughing.

"What's so funny?" Coach Ross asked him.

"I just showed them a Hawk's not a chicken!" Tony grinned. "A Hawk is faster than a chicken!"

The Butler boys had to believe that—they lost the game 34–14.

Now people were trying to figure out why Tony, who was supposed to be the worst of the Dorsett runners, was suddenly looking like the best. He was fast, and he could start quicker than most players. But his good running seemed to be more than that. Ed Wilamowski said, "Tony seems to have an extra sense. He knows when somebody is behind him, and he can get away when nobody else could."

It was almost as if Tony had a special antenna, one that picked up the sound of tacklers coming. No, Coach Ross said, it was his eyesight. Tony had extra good peripheral vision—he could be looking straight ahead and still see farther to both sides than most people could. Eye doctors were always surprised to find out how wide his range of vision was. He could see a flash of color way off to one side, make a fast cut, and get away.

His speed and vision combined with a natural feeling for playing football. As a Dorsett, he seemed to have been born with that, as well as the body control that all great athletes have. If he was knocked into the air, he knew exactly what position his body was in, and could come down on his feet, still running. His mother called that his sense of balance. Even as a baby, he could climb high places, and he never fell off.

Besides, nobody had ever just given him the ball and told him to run before!

Now Coach Ross wanted to make sure Tony used his

Tony had thin legs, but they were strong. Here he is making a long run against Beaver Falls, 1971. (*Photo courtesy Richard "Butch" Ross*)

talents, and used them in the right direction. "You have God-given abilities that other kids don't have," Ross told him. "But you have to work to develop them."

Ross wasn't really worried about Tony not working. Tony was one of the hardest workers on the squad. Coach Ross always said the only thing that discouraged Tony was to take him out of a scrimmage, and especially a game.

He saw that Tony was quick to learn, too. "He might make a mistake once," Ross said, "but never the same mistake twice!"

Knowing that, he talked to Tony about his grades, too. Tony had been an honor student in junior high, but his sophomore grades were not as good. They had been passing, but not high. "You might have a chance for a college football scholarship, but you have to have the grades, too," he said.

Tony looked at the ex-football stars standing on the street corner or hanging around the pool room. "Is that where you want to spend the rest of your life?" Ross asked the boys.

Tony knew he didn't want to be any has-been pool hustler. He wanted to make his family proud of him, and he wanted more than ever to do something for them. Maybe football would be the way—maybe he could use his strong legs to run away from that steel mill!

Tony saw what he had to do. He had two jobs—one on the football field and the other in the classroom. Now that he had a reason for working he put all his strength into it.

His teachers noticed that he was doing better in class, and his grades started coming up. But he was still shy about speaking up in class. "If you asked him a question," one teacher said, "he wouldn't answer right away. He would think it over for a while, but then he'd come up with the right answer."

On the football field, Tony wasn't shy, and he didn't have

to think about the right answer. His eyes took in the whole field on every play, and his feet were so quick they took him to the right place—wherever there was a hole to get through.

After a game, he remembered every play and analyzed it. The coaches around his mom's kitchen table did that, too. His brothers told him what he had done wrong, and how to do it better the next time.

In the next game, Tony did do it better. The Vikings had no trouble rounding up the Farrell Night Riders, and Tony showed them one of his patented runs when he took a handoff at his own 48. He flashed through the right side of the line, cut back toward the sideline and beat everybody to the goal line. He ended the day with 133 yards in only 13 carries as the Vikings won 45–0.

But, across the hill, the Aliquippa Indians were wearing new shirts. And stenciled on them were the words, "Beat Hopewell!"

The Hopewell-Aliquippa game was always a bruiser. The boys on the two teams were friends and neighbors who hung out together when they weren't pounding each other on a football field. They wanted to beat each other more than they wanted to beat any other team.

Coach Ross worked the team hard in practice. He had a funny feeling that things had been going too well. And in the first half it looked as if his fears might be coming true. Hopewell led at the end of the half, 14–6, but Aliquippa led in all the other statistics. In the locker room, Ross made some blocking changes. He warned the team they had been taking the Indians too lightly.

In the second half, the Viking defense came back and held the Indians to minus 32 yards rushing! The final score was 28–6. The key to the game, said the *Beaver County Times*, was Tony Dorsett, who rushed for 120 yards and scored two touchdowns.

TONY DORSETT

Tony hoped to be a key in the next game, too. McKeesport had beaten the Vikings 15–14 last year, and the Vikings were looking for a little revenge. Coach Ross had the team working on their passing game all week. "If we can throw on them, it'll loosen up our running game," he said.

With Tony averaging 9 yards a carry for the season, the running game didn't seem to need much more loosening up. Tony was confident, but not cocky, Coach Ross said. The whole team had that attitude, he thought, and that was the way he wanted them.

To outsiders, Tony did sometimes seem cocky, but at Hopewell they understood that. If Tony strutted or swaggered down the hall once in a while, his friends and teachers knew he was trying to cover up his shyness.

Tony didn't seem shy when he intercepted a pass on the 46-yard line against McKeesport and moved the ball in eleven plays to score.

After that, McKeesport fumbled on their own five, and the Vikings recovered. On the next play, Tony and two McKeesport players went in for the TD. The McKeesport boys were just along for the ride. They were hanging on to Tony's legs, and he showed his power by dragging them with him. The final was 21–14, Hopewell.

Well, back to blocking practice, said Coach Ross. He said the offensive blocking hadn't been exactly great in that game. And against New Castle next week it would have to be a lot better. The New Castle Hurricanes had lost only once, to Ambridge. They'd like nothing better than to knock the Vikings out of the playoffs!

For the first half, the Hurricanes thought they had found out how to stop Tony. They were leading 6–0. Then, at the end of the half, Tony took a quick pitch from Hummell on the New Castle 34. He followed his blocker through the right side of the line. Then he passed him.

TONY DORSETT

The overflow crowd was on its feet roaring and jumping as Tony crossed the goal line and the clock ran out.

Now leading 7–6, the Vikings came out of the locker room ready to turn the game around. On the second play, Tony took the ball on his own 22. He broke through the line and stumbled. But he didn't fall!

In one quick motion, he regained his balance and broke away from a tackle at the same time. Two more defenders were coming at him. He faked one into going the wrong direction, and spun around the other. At the 40, Tony went into high gear. You could almost see a jet trail behind him! He left the Hurricanes behind, too, and made the score 14–6.

After that, he got a 43-yard run to set up another TD. The Vikings won, 21–14, and Tony had run for 193 yards! The Viking fans mobbed Coach Ross and the players. Ross said, "This has to be one of the greatest days of my life. The team was just great. They gave a superb effort!"

New Castle coach Lindy Lauro said there was one thing that made the difference in the game—Tony Dorsett. "He's one of the best I've ever seen," he said. "We thought we could stop him, but he can run, catch, he plays good defense—he does everything!"

After the celebration, the team had to come back to earth again and realize the season wasn't over yet. There were two games left to play. Next week were the Sharon Bengals, who wouldn't be too tough, but the last one would be with Beaver Falls. The Vikings would have to be ready for that one. Beaver Falls was where Joe Namath had played his high school ball, and his coach, Larry Bruno, was still putting out good teams there.

As the team drove north to Sharon, they felt confident. But Tony felt miserable. He'd had tonsillitis all week. Still, nobody thought about having too much trouble with the Bengals--they had won only two games, and they'd lost eight.

Ed Wilamowski blocks for Tony against the Sharon Bengals. Randy Holloway is the Sharon player on the far right. (*Photo courtesy Richard "Butch" Ross*)

TONY DORSETT

But the game started off badly. The Bengals took the opening kickoff and marched 81 yards in 11 plays to score.

Coach Ross soon started thinking he was watching a nightmare. In the whole first quarter, Tony carried the ball four times, for a total of 4 yards. For the Hawk, that was the same as standing still.

Toward the end of the quarter, the Vikings held the Bengals at the 1-yard line. Alkey Hummell passed for 28 yards to get out of the hole.

But on the next play, Tony fumbled the ball. The Bengals recovered. Five plays later, they had another touchdown.

Tony wanted to make up for that fumble. The next time Sharon tried to pass, Tony dove to intercept it. But his timing was off tonight. He missed the ball and his head hit the ground. A teammate couldn't stop in time, and his foot accidentally hit Tony in the head.

Tony was knocked out!

When he came to, he was seeing lights and hearing bells. Coach Ross sat him on the bench, the thing Tony hated most. As awful as he felt, he tried to get the coach to put him back in.

Coach Ross said, "No." But he didn't have time to talk about it. The game was swinging back and forth like a ping-pong match. Sharon recovered another fumble, then the Vikings intercepted a pass. Then they fumbled again. Sharon recovered. Then the Vikings intercepted another pass. It was enough to make anybody dizzy.

With 4 seconds left in the half, the Vikings took over the ball on downs. But the clock hadn't stopped when both teams left the field. The visiting Hopewell band marched onto the field, but then weird things started happening.

The officials were blowing their whistles!

What? Were the band members offside? They didn't know, but they thought they must be, because the referees made them leave the field.

The band was dumbfounded. The players were so mixed up they didn't know which way to run. The referees told them to go back on the field. The fans thought everybody had gone crazy out there!

When it was all straightened out, the officials set the scoreboard clock back to 4 seconds and told Hopewell to start a play. Feeling shaky and confused, the Vikings tried a pass; it was incomplete. Finally, the teams got into the locker rooms.

But the Vikings couldn't get settled down to think about what to do in the second half. And Coach Ross had his hands full with Tony.

A Sharon doctor looked at Tony and told Ross, "Use your own judgment about playing him." That really put Ross on the spot. The team needed Tony now, and the fans wanted him back in the game. But Ross didn't know how badly Tony was injured. He didn't know whether he was weak from the tonsillitis and the medicine he'd been taking for it, or whether he might have a concussion.

Again, Ross said, "No! I won't risk any kid's career for just one game."

Did Tony want to go back in? Huh.

He was making so much noise about it that Coach Ross had to take him by the shoulders and get him out of the dressing room. He took him up the steps to another small room, away from the other boys.

Westley Dorsett came in then, to see what was wrong with Tony. He found Tony trying to tell Coach Ross that he was going back in the game!

"Sit down and listen to the coach," Mr. Dorsett ordered. When that quiet man spoke, Tony knew he had to listen.

So, as Sharon went on to win the game 19–6, Tony had to watch from the sidelines. It seemed like the worst night of his life. The WPIAL championship had just gone down the drain. Tony looked at the Sharon Bengals having their celebration. He didn't say anything, but he was thinking. He was thinking that he'd be back next year. The Bengals would see the Hawk in action again, and maybe they wouldn't enjoy it so much next time!

Coach Ross had to take a lot of heat for not putting Tony back in the game. And, disappointed as he was himself, he had to pull the team together and get them ready to play Beaver Falls. Luckily, the doctors' tests and X-rays showed that Tony's injury was not serious and they said he could play.

Even with one loss now, the Beaver Falls game wouldn't be an anticlimax. If they won this game, Hopewell would have its first MAC championship. If they lost, Beaver Falls would win it.

Tony came back this week like a streak. He ran for 112 yards in 22 carries. Hopewell won the MAC championship and the game, 23–7!

Ross was named MAC Coach of the Year, and Tony won almost all the honors a player could get. He led Beaver County in rushing with 1,034 yards and in scoring with 114 points. He was named to the MAC all-star team, was the MAC Most Valuable Player, and made first team All-State!

In spite of the loss to Sharon, it had been a great year for Tony and the whole team. And next year, the boys told each other, they'd win them all!

CHAPTER IV

Strangers were eyeing Tony. They were reading the press clippings and looking at his statistics. Their eyes were popping.

The football banquets and awards ceremonies were hardly over before Tony started hearing from these strangers. The strangers were college football coaches, and they all wanted Tony.

Letters and phone calls started coming from places like California, Colorado, and Florida. Tony was surprised to hear from schools so far away. Since he didn't know much about any of them, he just laid back and waited to see what would happen.

Now, college recruiters are allowed only three visits to a player's home, but in 1972 there was no limit on their visits. They came, and didn't want to leave until Tony promised to go to their school. Sometimes they stayed so long Mrs. Dorsett almost had to sweep them out of her spotless living room with her broom!

In the fall, so many coaches came to see Tony at school that his friends kidded him about it. They offered to sell tickets, or maybe make the coaches take numbers and stand in line!

Calls from recruiters kept Mr. Waters and Mr. Ross busy.

Tony as a high school star, starting his senior year. (*Photo courtesy Richard "Butch" Ross*)

But they thought it was exciting, and so did the rest of the school. One day Ohio State's famous coach, Woody Hayes, came stomping down the halls at Hopewell, and caused a stir that lasted for days. Kids were peeking around corners and doorways at him, and he excited the faculty by dropping into the teachers' room to lecture them on history.

Both Mr. Waters and Mr. Ross did their best to help Tony and the other players who were being recruited. They didn't tell them what to decide. But they did want to help them make good decisions about where to go to college. They talked with the boys many times about what kind of schools they would like. Mr. Waters sometimes screened out people he knew the boys didn't want to talk to.

At home, Mrs. Dorsett always talked to the recruiters with Tony. At school, Coach Ross would be with him. But if Mr. Ross was holding class, Tony would have to go to the guidance room alone.

The coaches all told him what a good football program they had, how many bowl games they had gone to, what a wonderful school their's was, what a good chance Tony would have to be a starter right away. . . .

Sometimes they started sounding like a broken record, all of them saying the same things over and over.

After talking to Tony, coaches would often ask Coach Ross, "Do you think I got through to him? He didn't seem to answer!"

Coach Ross wasn't surprised—he knew Tony. "Tony's like somebody buying a pair of shoes," he'd say. "He's trying you on!"

If all those meetings and phone calls caused an uproar around Hopewell, the football season caused more. Tony wanted a football scholarship, but right now he wanted something else. He wanted the Vikings to win the WPIAL championship. So did the rest of the team. If they got jealous of all the attention Tony was getting, it could wreck the season. But that never happened.

Although there were only four or five black players on the team, there was never any jealousy or infighting. The players went to the same parties and stayed together in school. They never felt there was a difference among them.

The only difference was that the Hawk could start quicker and run faster than anybody else. He always gave the team credit for the awards he won, and he didn't "act big" about them. If he had, the boys would just have told him to cut the jiving.

Any time Coach Ross was asked about Tony, he couldn't help smiling. "He's our big threat," he told reporters before the season started. "He has speed, moves, and something you can't teach a kid—football sense." Tony was a good blocker, too, he said, if anybody would just notice.

Ross was pleased with the way the whole team was looking. That outstanding group from Tony's sophomore year was now a senior team with plenty of experience. In the I-formation backfield with Tony were big Dan Rains, a good blocking fullback; quarterback Chuck Hoover, and Tony's old pal Mike Kimbrough. Mike was a good power runner who could take some of the pressure off Tony.

On defense, Tony was still playing monster. On pass rushes, most teams "rush four," or "rush seven." That is, they send either four or seven men through the line to get the passer. Many times, Hopewell rushed ten! Everybody but Tony would rush the passer. He dropped back to "play centerfield"—to catch or stop anybody who broke through. That would surprise the other teams—they didn't have anybody fast enough to try such a thing!

The Viking players knew they had a rough season ahead. But, against Ambridge, winning didn't look so hard. On the Vikings' first drive, Tony beat the right half of the Am-

Two good runners and good friends: Mike Kimbrough and Tony.
(*Photo courtesy Richard "Butch" Ross*)

bridge team around end and raced 14 yards for a touchdown. On the next series he broke two tackles and ran 33 yards.

After that, play settled down to the usual hard blocking and tackling. In the fourth quarter, Tony was shaken up on a tackle. "I'm thirty-five years old," Coach Ross said later, "and when he didn't get up right away, I felt like I was sixty-five!"

But Tony went back in, intercepted a pass, and ended the game with 103 yards in 16 carries as the Vikings won 19–6!

In the sad, quiet Ambridge locker room, there was a reporter who didn't seem to care how long his head stayed

Tony scores against Ambridge and says, "Hi!" to the band. (*Photo courtesy Richard "Butch" Ross*)

attached to his shoulders. "Why did your team lose the game?" he asked the Ambridge coach.

The coach said two words: "Anthony Dorsett."

In the noisy Hopewell locker room, Coach Ross was smiling and modest. "It was just Tony's usual great game," he said.

Tony played his usual great game again the next week, but only for the first half. Well, at the half the score was 35–6, Hopewell. Tony had already passed to Jeff Hineman for a touchdown, scored three times himself, and gained 127 yards. Coach Ross took pity on poor West Mifflin North and put in the second team. They scored 20 more points.

Against Ellwood City, which had already lost to Farrell and Butler, the Vikings put on another scoring show. In the first eight minutes, they had the ball only twice.

The first time, Tony had a 71-yard scoring run, with Ed Wilamowski running interference. The next time they had the ball, the Vikings scored on a long pass play from Hoover to Hineman.

As the Vikings won 41–14, Tony had 182 yards in only fourteen carries. The headline in the *Beaver County Times* said, "Pick a Complimentary Adjective—It Fits Dorsett." The sportswriter thought of a few: "Outstanding, fantastic, super, stellar, powerful, speedy, classy." Then he ran out of words, and so did Coach Ross. "There are just not enough adjectives to describe Dorsett," he said.

"They tried to stop Tony," he went on, "but there is no way to stop him." Coach Ross was just glad he didn't have to do it. "If I was coaching against him I'd be stumped," he said.

Up north in Butler they were staying up late trying to think of ways to stop him. Both teams were undefeated. Whoever won this game would probably win the MAC championship. They might go on to win the WPIAL, too, if they won the rest of their games. Or, as Coach Ross put it, "It's one game and you're out."

Pressure. That's what the strain to go undefeated meant. Ross felt it, the team felt it, and everybody in Hopewell High felt it. But Coach Ross didn't give any big locker room speeches about it. He didn't believe in rah-rahs. He believed in work.

The Vikings worked hard all week. They were set to try their hardest to beat Butler. But sometimes a team can try too hard. It makes them tight when they should be loose. And there's nothing like a rainstorm to mess everything up.

The rainstorm didn't keep the fans away. The bleachers at Hopewell were sold out early. Fans were hanging on the fences and standing on the hilltops around the field. But the muddy field had the coaches worried. From the opening kickoff, the game looked like a sliding and fumbling match.

The first time the Vikings had to punt, the slippery ball skittered only 14 yards. Butler was in close, and scored.

The Viking defense held them after that, but the offense was getting bogged down in the mud. Until the fourth quarter. Tony took a handoff from Chuck Hoover. But he didn't run. He passed to Jeff Hineman—36 yards to the Butler 40-yard line.

On the next play, he took another handoff and kept the ball. He slid out of one tackle and jerked away from another. Then he turned on the speed. Down the sideline he went—all the way! But the point after the touchdown failed, leaving the Vikings behind 7–6.

Then everything went wrong.

Butler came back and scored. Time was getting short. The mud was getting deeper. Everybody's hands were wet. The ball was like a jumping bean. Hopewell had three fumbles already, and so did Butler. Hopewell soon had four.

On the first play after Butler's touchdown, Tony took

Tony tries to fly over the Butler line. It wasn't enough to win the game. (*Photo courtesy Richard "Butch" Ross*)

the ball at his own 37-yard line. But the wet ball squirted out of his hands. Butler recovered.

By this time, the Vikings' legs were feeling like lead. Most of them were playing both offense and defense. But Butler was using two platoons—one team on offense and another on defense—so they were fresher. Playing against the two platoons was like playing two games at once. And from the 37, Butler scored again. The final was Butler 20, Hopewell 6.

Tony had gained 90 yards in fifteen carries, scored Hopewell's only TD, intercepted a pass, recovered a fumble, and thrown the Vikings' longest pass completion. Still, Butler coach Art Bernardi was satisfied. He said his team had done a good job of shutting Dorsett off!

Coach Ross didn't make any excuses after the game. He said, "They simply outplayed us. They got an early TD and we had to play their game."

A reporter wrote about "the eerie gloom of the losers' dressing room." He said it was like a tomb in there. One of the players said, "Well, if you want to see a bunch of big boys break down and cry, this is the place!"

It was a game the Vikings couldn't do anything but cry about—and replay over and over before they went to sleep. It was still the first month of the season, and they'd already lost their chance for the WPIAL championship!

Coach Ross told them they couldn't let it get them down. They still had a chance to win the MAC championship again, but they'd have to come back like winners.

CHAPTER V

The Vikings weren't finished yet.

The next week they marched all over the Farrell Night Riders. Tony had two TD's as the Vikings won, 21–0.

It didn't make them feel better to find out that Beaver Falls was beating Butler 11–6, but Butler's losing gave them a better chance for the MAC title. *If* the Vikings could keep winning!

Next were the Aliquippa Indians, who were planning a defense to keep Tony in one position—flat on the ground. Everytime Tony tried to run outside, five or six Indians were there to meet him.

Coach Ross quickly changed strategy. He sent Tony running into the middle. The Hawk didn't break any long runs, but he was chewing up yardage on short ones. The Indian defense was good, but Tony was better. He gained 103 yards, but it took thirty-one carries to do it. That was twice his usual number of carries and the coaches worried about using him too much.

Tony didn't think it was too much. He was willing to carry the ball on every play if they asked him to. And beating Aliquippa, 26–12, was worth taking a little beating for!

Next week was an open date anyway, and, with no game coming up, Tony could rest for a few days. The Vikings all

Number 33 on defense in a 1972 game. Coach Ross said Tony played hard, tough defense. (*Photo courtesy Richard "Butch" Ross*)

relaxed, but they relaxed almost too much. They were playing New Castle, and you couldn't relax against that team!
The Vikings seemed rusty as they started the game. Their
timing was bad. At the half, they were behind 12–0. Coach
Ross took them into the locker room and shut the door.
He didn't often yell at them, but this time he chewed them
out. "If you're any kind of championship team you'll come
back and win!" he thundered.

Reporter Rich Emert watched the Viking comeback, and
he had to stretch his imagination to describe it. "You could
see it coming, just like the building of a thunderstorm," he
wrote. "First it starts to sprinkle, then it begins to rain
slowly, then it pours, and finally everything breaks loose.
That's exactly what happened last night in New Castle,
only it didn't rain water, it rained Hopewell Vikings!"

Tony hit New Castle more like a hailstorm. First he got
a 14-yard run for a TD. Then, as New Castle was threaten-
ing to score, he intercepted a pass on his own 20. He shifted
behind a blocker, and accelerated. If the Pittsburgh Ballet
had seen his fancy steps, they would have tried to hire him.
Picking up blockers along the way, he scored an 80-yard
touchdown!

The Vikings went on to win the game but, after the
celebration, a funny look came over Tony's face. It was a
look that was hard to figure out. But the Vikings knew
what it meant. It meant that the Sharon Bengals were coming to Hopewell next week.

Butch Ross kept a close eye on Tony. He could see the
determination building up in him all week. Tony didn't say
very much, but he practiced with more intensity than ever.
"I'm going to be around for the end of this one," he told
Ross.

Ross knew how badly Tony wanted to beat Sharon. He
made some changes in blocking assignments to try to help
him get loose. He figured Tony's own determination would

do the rest. He was right. The Bengals never knew what hit them.

On the first play from scrimmage, Tony threw a pass, 29 yards to Hineman. Two plays later, he broke a tackle and ran 15 yards to score. So much for the warm-up.

Next, he took a handoff on his own 33. He slid around left end, whooshed past a defender and jetted down the sideline for a 67-yard TD!

Was that enough? No.

On a draw play, Tony was stopped at the line of scrimmage. But when the Bengals looked in the pile-up, he wasn't there! He was 65 yards downfield, scoring another TD!

Tony ended the game with four touchdowns, of 15, 67, 65, and 16 yards. Besides that, he intercepted a pass, threw a touchdown pass, and set a new Beaver County rushing record with 247 yards in twenty-one carries!

Dorsett's revenge was something the Bengals hoped they would never see again. The only thing they had to celebrate was the fact that Tony Dorsett was graduating!

Graduating. That thought was going to make the next game a little sad—it would be Tony's last one for Hopewell. He and his buddies would never play together again.

But they didn't want to think about that yet. This game would be against Beaver Falls. Not much depended on it— only the MAC championship. Beaver Falls was undefeated. If they won, they would go into the WPIAL playoffs. But if Hopewell could win, the two teams would have identical records and would tie for the MAC championship.

From the opening kickoff, the game was all Hopewell. In the last quarter, the score was 28–0. With five minutes left to play, Tony took the ball. He was 64 yards from the goal line. He took off. His feet looked like they weren't even touching the ground. He ran through the whole Beaver Falls team—all the way, for his last high school touchdown.

In the end zone, he did a little dance, like he'd seen the pros do on TV.

As he trotted back to the bench, the crowd gave him a thundering, standing ovation. But Coach Ross looked at him sideways. "Hey," he called to Tony. "Hey, hot dog!"

Tony knew Coach Ross didn't like his players showing off like that. "We think we just have a little bit of class," he always told them.

Tony gave him a sheepish grin. "Coach," he said quickly, "before you get mad, let me tell you—the guys dared me to do that dance if I broke anything over 50 yards. They said I wouldn't have enough guts to do it!"

Coach Ross didn't mind it too much. "All those games, all the points he scored, and he never did anything like that before," he said. "And he did it just to satisfy his buddies."

In the locker room, there were a lot of misty eyes. Reporters crowded around Tony and Coach Ross. Ross told them, "I have had the opportunity of coaching Tony and I consider myself very, very fortunate. A player like him comes along once in a lifetime." And then he gave Tony his highest compliment: "If my son were to grow up and be the caliber of boy Tony is, I would be a very happy man."

The reporters jolted Tony back to real life by asking him where he planned to go to college. He'd been putting off thinking about that big decision, and now it was facing him already.

He answered slowly. "I want to stay close to home, but I want to go to a big school." He said he hoped the people who had helped him and followed his career at Hopewell would get a chance to watch him in college, and maybe even the pros.

Before Tony had to make that big choice about college, there were more honors coming to him. He took all the Beaver County and MAC scoring and rushing honors again,

TONY DORSETT

was named to the MAC all-star team, and was Most Valuable Player again, too. He was All-State on *both* offense and defense. And the big one came when he was named an All-American by *Parade* magazine!

At a special school assembly, Tony's number 33 jersey was retired. In honor of Tony's achievements, nobody at Hopewell would ever wear the Dorsett 33 again. Coach Ross said he just hoped he could live long enough to see Tony's jersey retired again, in college.

Now Tony had to get serious about where he would go to college. If only he could look into the future, and see what would work out best! But he just had to look, and listen, and judge for himself right now.

There was one school that fit the requirements he had talked about after the Beaver Falls game. It was close to home, his friends and family could come and see him play

Mr. John Waters, Hopewell High School principal, and Coach Ross at the special assembly retiring Tony's number 33. (*Photo courtesy Richard "Butch" Ross*)

there, and it was a big school. That school was the University of Pittsburgh and it was less than an hour's drive out the parkway from Aliquippa.

But Tony wanted to play for a winning team, too. And in Aliquippa, Pitt's football team wasn't rated much above the Sharon Bengals!

Right now, Pitt was having the worst season in its history. They had just finished losing ten games.

One or two local boys were playing at Pitt now, and they almost hated to come home. Aliquippa was such a football-minded town that the people didn't have any patience with losers. If they saw a Pitt football player on the street, they stopped him and demanded, "What's wrong with Pitt?" Little boys would yell, "You guys are no good!"

Tony didn't want that kind of hassle. He didn't have anything against Pitt. He just wished they knew how to play football over there. A school that hadn't had a winning season in ten years didn't seem like a place to build a career.

Maybe he'd be better off at Ohio State. It was always a football power and it was only about three hours away. Woody Hayes had made its football program sound exciting.

Tony was also thinking about Penn State, which was noted for putting out both winning teams and good pro players. But Penn State coach Joe Paterno hadn't come around, and he didn't seem interested in Tony.

The NCAA rules said that a high school player could accept free trips to six colleges. Tony enjoyed a few of these trips and found the schools all nice, and the players and coaches friendly. They always showed the recruits a good time. That just made the decision harder.

Coach Ross helped the boys to know what to look for on these trips. "Don't just talk to the coaches," he told them. "Talk to the ballplayers. Find out how they are treated." He also warned them, "You might like the coach who is recruiting you, but if he's a line coach and you play in the backfield he wouldn't be coaching you."

After a trip, Tony would sit down with Coach Ross and talk it over. Tony usually said, "They have a good program, Coach."

But sometimes, like a pair of shoes, he tried on a school and found it didn't fit. Once he told Ross, "That coach is a phony."

"He wouldn't say that to degrade the person," Ross explained. "That was just what came through to him."

Sometimes a coach would make too many promises, and Tony felt he couldn't believe him. Some coaches talked so much about playing defense that Tony crossed them off his list. He didn't want to play defense in college. He liked to carry the ball.

Tony and Ed Wilamowski were invited to visit Notre Dame. They were excited about that. "Notre Dame is Football, U.S.A.," Tony said.

When they came back, Coach Ross took one look at their long faces and said, "What's wrong?"

"They told us we were too small to play for Notre Dame," the boys said.

Even Ed, who was 6 feet, 4 inches tall, wasn't big enough. He only weighed 185 pounds. And Tony, well, "I heard they said I was just a skinny little kid who couldn't make it in big time football," he said.

Notre Dame hadn't heard about Dorsett's revenge, not yet. . . .

CHAPTER VI

T hings were going on at the University of Pittsburgh, things Tony didn't know about yet. One of them was indigestion.

The 1972 Pitt football season had given more people stomach aches and heartburn than the kielbassa (Polish sausage) that Pittsburghers are famous for eating. After suffering through one win and ten losses, university officials decided to make some changes. Their ulcers demanded changes, and so did the Pitt alumni.

The Pitt fans weren't greedy. If they got what they wanted for Christmas this year it would be, well, maybe to win *two* football games in the same season.

Pitt fans had pride. After all, their school had been playing football since 1890. Pitt teams had won no less than eight national championships. But the last one of those had been in 1937, and school spirit had sunk so low now that students didn't even want to wear Pitt Panther T-shirts around campus. If they did, people laughed at them.

But Santa Claus was coming.

A week before Christmas, he was flying into Pittsburgh, straight from the Liberty Bowl in Memphis, Tennessee. Santa Claus spoke with a southern accent, and he looked like a clean-cut former All-American football player. That's just what he was. Santa's real name was Johnny Majors, and he was the new Pitt head football coach.

After turning Iowa State's losing football team into a winner, Majors was becoming known as a miracle worker. But he had looked over the Pitt football program and he wasn't promising any miracles. "We've got to be realistic here," he was saying, "this isn't going to be easy."

Majors sent his assistants out in all directions. "Find me some players who hate to lose!" he told them.

That was one quality he wanted in his players. But he needed more than that. There was some doubt on campus as to whether the football team could beat the Pitt professors in a running race. The team needed speed. If Johnny Majors could bring the Pitt team what it needed most for Christmas, it would be a good, fast running back.

He knew where to look for that. Majors came to Pittsburgh on December 19th. On the 20th, he was in Aliquippa.

Coach Foge Fazio, an assistant coach at Pitt, was from Ambridge. He and Butch Ross had been friends for a long time. He called and said, "Butch, would you have Ed Wilamowski and Tony Dorsett come over to your house? I'll bring Coach Majors there."

"Sure," Coach Ross said.

"Why not?" said Ed and Tony. But they didn't think they'd be impressed. They had seen Coach Majors on TV the night before, and they wondered what language he was talking. It didn't sound like anything they'd ever heard in Aliquippa!

But, after all, he was coming to see them on his second day in town. And they had listened to so many other coaches, they thought they might as well hear what this one had to say.

Mrs. Ross had done her Christmas baking, and she had a great spread of nut rolls, cookies, and other goodies on her dining room table. Ed and Tony settled down there and munched happily.

Then Johnny Majors walked in and started talking. He didn't stop for two hours. The first thing he said was, "You are the two I want to build my program on at Pitt!"

Mrs. Ross moved in and out of the dining room, bringing more cookies and her special Italian punch. The two small Ross children sat very still, with their eyes getting bigger and bigger. Tony and Ed kept sitting up farther and farther on their chairs, trying to figure out what Majors was saying!

He talked so fast their ears couldn't seem to keep up with him. He seemed to turn his sentences around and slur them together in funny ways. The boys were always about a paragraph behind his Tennessee accent. Finally, they just gave up and fixed their eyes on his face. Once they looked at each other and smiled, because they realized what they were doing. Both of them were trying to read his lips!

But they liked the parts they could understand. "You're going to be part of something new, something exciting," Majors told them. "I want people who hate to lose. We will play with pride, enthusiasm, and intensity. We will *learn how to win!*"

The boys felt a little dazed, but Majors didn't give them time to clear their heads. Pitt was a famous university, he told them. Dr. Jonas Salk had developed the polio vaccine there. They would play football in an atmosphere of learning. They would come out with a good education.

"You can be a part of building something at Pitt," he went on. "You will have the opportunity to play on a national championship team!" The boys had to smile at that one.

"The player comes first in our organization," Majors promised. "We will look after you for four years." They would have a good chance of playing as freshmen, too, he said. At other schools, they might have to wait longer.

TONY DORSETT

Majors's enthusiasm was catching. Mrs. Ross said, "Tony, if you don't sign up, I will!"

But Tony and Ed still wanted to think about it. They didn't have to decide till May, and they weren't ready to say anything yet.

Coach Majors wouldn't give up on them, though. After that first visit, he came back at least once a week. He assigned Jackie Sherrill, his assistant head coach, to Hopewell. Sherrill was there so much that the boys would jokingly ask him if he slept in the school gym at night!

Tony and Ed liked Coach Sherrill. He talked straight, and he really seemed to care about them. Sherrill was born in Oklahoma, went to high school in Mississippi, and had played football at the University of Alabama, so the boys had trouble with his accent, too. When Sherrill asked them a question, they'd answer it and then hope it was the right answer. They were often afraid they had answered the wrong question!

Other coaches hadn't given up, either. Frank Kush came from Arizona State. Finally Joe Paterno came too, but Tony and Ed looked at each other and shook their heads. They had heard that Penn State thought they were too small, or maybe that their grades weren't good enough. Now they thought he had come too late.

So many coaches were coming that Tony complained to Jackie Sherrill that he didn't even have a chance to eat lunch. Sherrill smiled, and called his mother, in Biloxi, Mississippi. She came to Pittsburgh and baked an old-fashioned rhubarb pie for Tony.

"Man, that pie was good!" Tony said. He claimed he had to fight his mother for the last piece of it.

Tony wouldn't make up his mind because of a rhubarb pie, but other things were pushing him toward making a decision. Recruiting was a little like that pie—it was great at first. But if somebody kept stuffing it in your mouth and making you eat it day after day, you'd soon get sick of it. It was just too much of a good thing.

The boys kept thinking they should talk to more coaches, but when they did they only felt more mixed-up. They knew that no matter what they decided, it could be wrong. Their whole futures were at stake here and, after all, they were only eighteen years old. They knew they were too green. But soon, they were going to have to trust somebody.

Ed made a decision first—he was going to sign with a small college in Ohio. But then Coach Ross pulled him aside. "Is that what you really want to do?" he asked.

"Yes," Ed said. "I don't think I could play at a big school —Pitt or Penn State or anywhere like that."

"Well, take my advice for what it's worth," the coach said, "but I think you can play football on a larger scale than you're giving yourself credit for."

Ed tossed that around for a while, and finally in February, he and Tony sat down together and started talking. "Well, what are you thinking?" Ed asked.

"What are *you* thinking?" Tony said.

They both wanted to go to school with at least one of the other Vikings. But Ed hadn't said anything to Tony before, because he didn't want to hold him back. Tony had a scholarship offer from Ohio State, but Ed didn't. If Tony wanted to go there, Ed didn't want to say anything to change his mind.

Slowly, as they talked, their feelings came out. They found out that neither of them wanted to go away from home. They wanted their families to see them play. They wanted to stay together, and if anything went wrong, they wanted to be able to get home.

Before long, they saw they were both thinking about Pitt.

At Pitt, they thought they'd have the best chance of starting in their first year. But Tony, especially, would be taking a big chance. If he went to Ohio State or Southern California, he'd have the big, experienced offensive linemen in front of him. Pitt's offense last year had scored only 193 points in eleven games, while their opponents ran off with 350. Tony could be out there all alone. Without protection, he could get slaughtered.

But there was something else to think about, too. At one of those powerhouse schools he'd have to get in line behind a lot of other running backs. At Ohio State, Archie Griffin was already burning up the field, and he'd just be a sophomore. Tony didn't want to wait till Archie Griffin graduated. He didn't want to sit on the bench.

Finally, Ed and Tony said to each other, "What the heck, we might as well make a go at it."

They talked to Coach Ross first. If they signed anything, they wanted him to be there to make sure it was all right. Then they told Coach Sherrill and Coach Majors they were coming to Pitt. The coaches were elated. With Coach Ross, the boys went over to Pitt for a press conference and were interviewed on TV.

The boys were relieved to have the big decision made. Pitt's assistant coaches out on their recruiting trips were happy, too. Now they could tell other players that an All-American, the best running back in Pennsylvania, maybe the best in the country, was coming to Pitt. Tony's name helped to bring in other good recruits.

Tony then went out for track to start getting in shape. On the next day he was entered in the 50-yard dash in an indoor meet in Pittsburgh. He wasn't happy with his performance there. He almost broke a record which had stood for fifty years in that event, but he only tied it.

The next morning, Mr. Waters stopped him in the hall. "What happened, Tony?" he grinned. "You slowing down?"

Tony looked at him seriously, worried. "I don't know," he said. "I had trouble starting out of those blocks!"

"Tony!" Mr. Waters laughed. "If you'd had any practice

starting out of the blocks, you'd have broken the record, not tied it!"

Even at track meets coaches were still hounding Tony. Although he had announced that he was going to Pitt, other coaches were still trying to talk him out of it. Some of them acted a little rough.

When Tony told one coach he wasn't going to his school because he wanted to start in his freshman year, the coach yelled at him, "What makes you think you can start for us? What makes you think you're good enough?"

Sometimes a coach would try to get him by himself, outside the school, and try to trick him into signing papers. But Tony always said he wouldn't do anything unless Coach Ross was there and approved it.

Right up to "letter of intent" day in May, rival coaches kept telling Tony what a big mistake he was making in going to Pitt. By the time Tony was supposed to sign his letter to go to Pitt, he was so hurt, nervous, upset and angry that he disappeared!

Coach Sherrill went to see Tony run in a track meet, but Tony wasn't there. He had turned in his uniform.

The track coach came to Sherrill and demanded, "Where is Tony?"

But Sherrill didn't know, and neither did his brother, who had come to watch him run, too.

Sherrill started looking for him. It wasn't till late that night that he found him, hiding out with friends. Sherrill took him home, and spent the rest of the night sitting in his car outside Tony's house. He wasn't letting another coach get in to see Tony now!

Early the next morning, Tony and Ed signed their letters. With that finally done, Tony could settle down and think about graduation. After that came the "Big 33" game, an all-star game with the best high school players in Pennsylvania against the best from Ohio. It would be played in

TONY DORSETT

Hershey, Pennsylvania, where the air smelled like chocolate and the stands were thick with college coaches.

The college coaches were there to look over their new recruits. Johnny Majors was keeping an eye on two of his—Carson Long, a kicker, and Tony Dorsett. So far, he had never seen Tony play. He had watched his high school films, but he was anxious to see him on the field.

In Hershey, Tony had his first taste of talking with a lot of reporters he didn't know. He didn't like it much, but he gave them a taste of his honesty, too. "Do you think you can do in college what you did in high school?" That was the question they all wanted to ask him.

"I think I can make it," Tony answered simply. He didn't know how much Johnny Majors was hoping he would make it, too.

Tony played a good game. It wasn't his "usual great game," but he gained 61 yards rushing and caught passes for 54 more. And when he ran, well, he ran. He broke tackles. He ran what looked like full speed in one direction, then suddenly cut back and doubled his speed in the other direction.

Majors, sitting with other college coaches, didn't say anything. He waited till he got back to his motel room and shut the door behind him. Then he let out a real rebel yell. "Hallelujah!" he yelled. "We have us a running back!"

Only a day later, August 20th, it was time to report to Pitt for fall camp. Tony decided not to go.

CHAPTER VII

After the Big 33 game, Tony was tired. He felt bruised. He didn't like strangers asking him questions all the time. And, after all the years of wanting to get out of the project, of hoping and planning for something better, when the time came Tony just didn't want to leave home.

But then he looked up the street to the poolroom and down Franklin Avenue to the mill. He knew if he stayed that was where he was going.

"If I had quit then," Tony said later, "I'd probably be just another person out on the concrete."

So, a little shaky and lonely and doing his best to hide it, Tony turned away from home and went to Pittsburgh.

It wasn't a long drive from Aliquippa to Pittsburgh, but it was like going to a whole new world for Tony. Taking the Oakland exit from the Parkway East brought him out onto Forbes Avenue. Suddenly, straight ahead, was the university's main building, the Cathedral of Learning. Its towering gothic architecture made everything else seem very small, especially a young football player who was already feeling homesick.

Looking left from Forbes Avenue, just a couple of blocks up the hill, was Pitt Stadium. It was surprising to see it there, sitting right in the city among hospitals and university buildings. Tony might feel at home there, some day. Then again, he might not. . . .

For the next three days, he was sure he never would feel at home. It was check in, weigh in, go to the doctor, go to the stadium, go to the dorm, go to your advisor. There was always somebody saying, "Do this, do that, say this, say that, eat now, don't eat now. . . ." It was a zoo.

Finally, it was, "Get on the bus."

The team took the bus to the University of Pittsburgh at Johnstown, a Pitt campus in the mountains east of Pittsburgh. Another new place, and more confusion.

On the first day, Pitt's Sports Information Director Dean Billick saw Tony trying to unlock the door of his dormitory room. He had a pair of glasses pushed down on the end of his nose and a big floppy hat pulled down around his ears.

"What's the trouble?" Billick asked.

"This key won't fit," Tony complained.

Billick looked at the key and then smiled. "You're in the wrong building," he said kindly.

"Thanks," Tony muttered. He felt stupid, and he hated it. He sauntered away, trying to act laid-back, cool, because some reporters were watching.

The reporters looked at each other as if to say that Pitt had just placed bets on a losing horse. After Tony had gone, they laughed, "*That's* supposed to be the savior of Pitt football?"

Tony stayed cool, almost too cool. He was so quiet the other players, except for Ed, thought he was unfriendly. He walked around by himself and he ate by himself, watching everybody with his Hawk's eyes and waiting to see how things would go.

The Johnstown campus was like a resort, with stone buildings among big trees. Looking down over the mountains, a person could see almost to Aliquippa. But, in this beautiful setting, Tony felt strange and alone. He wouldn't talk to anybody about that, though. If he had, he would have found out that most of the other players felt as nervous as he did.

The last year before a new NCAA rule about scholarships went into effect was 1973. Now, a team can give only thirty scholarships a year. But that year there were eighty-four new players. And nobody knew which ones would make it.

Coach Majors and his new staff had to test them all and, as coaches say, "find the football players." Majors said, "We have to find out who can block, who can run, who can catch!"

He had to sort out the ones who would fit best into his system of play, and he had to know which ones were willing to work hard enough to do it. His way of sifting them out was to start them off working harder than they had ever worked before.

Practice started early in the morning. Running. The boys ran, practiced blocking, and ran. Then they ran up steps and through an obstacle course, learned plays, and ran some more. When they were so tired they thought they couldn't move, they started running again.

In the afternoon, they started over. They had sprint drills, in which the winner moved up a group, and the loser moved down. There were group sprints. If one of the group didn't finish in the given time, the whole group had to do it over.

Then there was the little matter the coaches smilingly called "country fair." The coaches were stationed around the field. Each of them had instructions for a different drill or exercise. The players moved from one coach to another, doing stretching exercises with one, weight lifting with another, and on, and on.

One thing was making everything harder—the weather. It was *hot*. And humid. Nobody could remember hotter weather for football camp. Pounds were pouring off the players, along with the sweat. That was good for some of the big linemen, but Tony didn't have pounds to spare.

At night, the players fell into bed and groaned. But their rooms were so hot they couldn't sleep. Finally, most of them picked up their mattresses and took them over to the air-conditioned gym. That's where they slept, with their mattresses scattered on the floor. It looked like a disaster relief shelter.

At the end of the first week, Majors called the first scrimmage. If that scrimmage had been a TV show, it would have been "The Three Stooges." But Johnny Majors wasn't laughing.

He stomped along the sideline, growling at whatever fate had given him this bunch of left-footed comedians who were out there dropping balls, tripping over their own feet, banging their heads on the ground, and blocking the wrong man.

He put the first team offense against the second team defense. The offense ran twenty plays in a row. If they scored, they took the ball back and started over.

Billy Daniels was playing quarterback. He was a junior, and he had experience. After all, he'd started a game . . . once. Behind him was a new tailback, wearing number 33, who was running for 5 or 6 yards at a time.

Somebody hissed at Ed Wilamowski: "When's he going to break one?"

"Don't worry about it. He will," Ed said.

It took about fifteen plays. Then Daniels called for a screen pass. A linebacker was about 10 feet away when Tony caught the ball. The linebacker thought he had an easy tackle. But in the second it took him to get there, the tailback disappeared. The linebacker turned around and watched Tony cross the goal line all alone—75 yards away!

"Who," the linebacker said with a shocked look on his face, "is number 33?"

Other people were wearing shocked looks, too. They were the coaches. They looked at each other and rolled their eyes as if to say, "Hmmm . . . that ain't bad!"

The coaches had all thought Tony was going to be good. In fact, the defensive coaches had lost an argument that he ought to be on the defensive team. For the defense, they wanted players who were aggressive and reckless, who had fast reactions. Offensive players couldn't be reckless—they had to stay calm and carry out their assignments, no matter what happened.

But great athletes could play either offense or defense, and the coaches of both sides thought Tony was a great athlete. At the same time, they didn't want to count too much on a freshman. Too many high school stars could never make the big change from high school to major college football. Tony's run had just raised their hopes.

Number 33 himself was feeling good. Running like that was like flying. It made him feel free, happy. And he knew he had shown something to these colleges dudes. He was always nervous about talking to them—he never knew what to say. But now his feet were talking.

Well, it might have been a lucky run. Tony figured he'd have to do a little more convincing. On the next series, he was tackled. *No!* He jerked away from the tackle and flew downfield for another touchdown!

Next, the call sent him toward the center of the hulking defensive line. A surprised guard and tackle saw only a blur as Tony slid between them and took off again. Both squads followed him, cheering.

Now Johnny Majors was smiling. In fact, he was jumping up and down like a prospector who's just discovered gold. He was so excited he raced halfway down the field after Tony, but he couldn't catch up with him, either.

TONY DORSETT

After that day, nobody had to ask who number 33 was. But Tony still had not played a real college game. And Pitt's first opponents, the Georgia Bulldogs, sent word up north that they had a vicious bite.

CHAPTER VIII

Tony was homesick.

When camp was over, he took off for Aliquippa. He wanted to quit.

He didn't tell many people he was quitting, not even Coach Ross. He knew what Ross would say, He'd say Tony couldn't quit now, not after all the hard work he'd put in, all the people who were counting on him. . . . Tony didn't want to disappoint Coach Ross.

He didn't want to disappoint his mother, either. She told him, "If you quit, it will break my heart. But you'll be hurting yourself more than anyone else."

Tony knew she was right. His feet and his heart were dragging, but he went back to Pitt.

Tony was back on the practice field, and there his feet never dragged. Every time he broke a play, he sprinted to the goal line. He didn't have to do that. Usually in practice the play just stopped when it passed the line of scrimmage.

Running for a touchdown even in practice was a habit Tony had started in high school. He wanted to get the feeling of always going for that goal line, from any place on the field. Coach Ross said it was just another example of the extra effort Tony always put into his work.

It surprised the Pitt coaches at first, but they liked it. It got the rest of the offense fired up. Before long, they started running for the goal line with Tony.

The coaches were hoping that Tony would be a leader, but they hadn't told him that. He was smart enough to figure it out for himself. He and Coach Ross had talked about it last year—what it meant to be a team leader. Ross told him the best way was to lead by your actions, not by yelling and screaming. "If you're going to be a team leader, you lead by your ability out on the field—you *show* the other people," he said.

That was one reason Tony always tried to work harder in practice than anybody else. It wasn't that he loved to practice. He didn't. But he knew what would happen if he goofed off. Other players would do it, too. They'd start saying, "Tony doesn't have to do it—why should I?"

Almost every day, Tony stayed after practice to run. *Extra effort.* Johnny Majors, who had been a great running back himself at Tennessee, knew that Tony's running ability was natural. Coaches say you can't teach somebody to run, and Majors knew there was little they could show Tony that he couldn't already do. "Don't overcoach him," he grinned to Harry Jones, the offensive backfield coach. "Just be sure he gets on the team bus on Saturday!"

And that dreaded Saturday with the Georgia Bulldogs was coming up fast. Majors drilled the team hard, and wished for just one more week to get ready. There were too many ragged edges yet.

The Pitt fans were starting to get nervous stomachs again. One loyal fan decided he couldn't even listen to the game on the radio. He was going to a movie instead, to keep from having a nervous breakdown.

In Pittsburgh, the fans don't take football seriously—not much. They take it only a little more seriously than they would, say, World War III. Right now they were ready to give Majors and his new team a chance. They were behind him all the way—until he failed. If Pitt looked bad against Georgia, they could turn on him in a hurry. They could go back to acting like the up-and-coming Steelers were the only team in town. There were even rumors going around that if Majors failed, Pitt might have to drop football!

But Johnny Majors was pushing optimism. "I never went into a game I thought I couldn't win," he said. One time his smile slipped, though, and he said to a sportswriter, "I'd like to know how we could come out of Georgia without getting annihilated!"

Even the Georgia coach, Vince Dooley, called the game "a venture into the unknown." The unknown was Pitt. It wasn't enough that the Pitt Panthers had that bad record to overcome; they also had at least a dozen first and second stringers who had never played in a college game before. And a new running back who was supposed to be fast, but had never faced a big college defensive line. He was so well-known around town that his name, said one Pittsburgh newspaper, was "Tony Dorsey."

Georgia, on the other hand, was expected to be among the top twenty teams in the country. As game time approached, Georgia was rated to beat Pitt by 15 points. At least. Sending what the papers were calling "Pitt's teen-agers" down into that tough Southeastern Conference seemed no more dangerous to Pitt fans than dropping them by parachute into North Vietnam.

On game day, September 15th, the Pitt campus was quiet, waiting. In Athens, Georgia, it was not quiet. As the Pitt team ran out on the field, the roar from 52,000 red-shirted Bulldog fans almost knocked them over. Tony had hardly been this far away from home before, and the noise nearly scared him to death. And what was that they were yelling? *"Dog meat! Dog meat!"*

Grrr. Their stomachs were churning their breakfasts into

butter, but the Pitt boys couldn't wait to get started. The Star Spangled Banner seemed to last about 45 minutes.

The Panthers' nervousness lasted till the hitting started. On the first series, Pitt forced the Bulldogs to punt. Then the Panthers took the ball on their own 39-yard line. The Panthers looked sharp in their new uniforms, with gold helmets, gold pants, and white jerseys trimmed in blue. Their play looked sharp, too.

Quarterback Billy Daniels pitched out to the left, to Tony. He got short yardage. And did it again, and again. First down. Hey, he could move against these Dogs!

Pitt was using the I-formation, with Tony at tailback behind junior fullback Dave Janasek. With Janasek's blocking, Tony kept picking up short runs. Mixing those with short passes to the ends, Pitt was moving down the field.

When they reached the 17-yard line, Daniels faked out the Dogs. He pitched out again to Tony. At least that's what the Dogs thought. By the time they found out Tony didn't have the ball, Daniels himself was crossing the goal line with it! Carson Long kicked the extra point and Pitt was leading, 7–0!

It wasn't until the second quarter that the Bulldogs broke through to score. Now it was 7–7. After that, both teams moved up and down the field, but couldn't score. Tony's running was moving the ball enough to keep the Bulldogs back in their own territory. And the defense was making them stay there.

By the fourth quarter, the Georgia heat seemed as vicious as the Bulldogs. But the Panthers were holding up well. Now they knew the reason for that tough training up in Johnstown. Compared to the Panthers, the Bulldogs were starting to look like a bunch of wilted daisies. Their own fans were starting to boo them.

With three minutes to go, a Panther drive stalled at the

Georgia 19. Carson Long came in to try a field goal. He kicked it high . . . and wide. The game ended, still 7–7. A tie was disappointing, but Pitt had *almost* won the game. The Panthers led all the statistics, and they had proved something. As Russ Franke wrote in *The Pittsburgh Press*, "Johnny Majors is for real."

And Tony, with 101 yards rushing, had proved he could play with the big boys.

Pitt fans walked around for the next week with their feet not quite touching the ground. That was all right for the fans, but not for the team. They were doing the same thing, still talking about the great game they'd played. They figured they could beat Baylor next week, easy!

But on Saturday, with only 28,000 fans rattling around in 56,000-seat Pitt Stadium, Pitt's defense was rattling around on the field. After handling Georgia, they couldn't stop the Baylor running game now. One reason was that middle guard Gary Burley, who had stomped the Georgia offense, was limping around on the sidelines with a bad ankle. But Johnny Majors was muttering something else. It sounded like "bonehead football."

With Pitt trailing 14–0 at the start of the third quarter, Tony took off. He weaved his way through tacklers who kept looming up at him, and missing him. He ran for 32 yards, and had his first college touchdown.

Tony ended the game with 121 yards, but it wasn't enough. Pitt lost the game 20–14. "We have a lot of work to do next week," Johnny Majors said. The team knew what he meant, and sighed.

A reporter asked Tony what had gone wrong. He gave his usual honest answer. "The whole team is to blame for the loss," he said. "Everybody thought we had an easy game coming up."

Nobody thought about easy games the next week. Tony worked hard with Janasek, his chief blocker, and he kept on running to the goal line. The coaches were watching him with squinty eyes. All right, he'd had two good games of more than a hundred yards. So far he'd looked good, but not great. They still couldn't tell how good he was going to be. The game this week with Northwestern might tell them more about that. By now, Tony wasn't going to be a surprise to anybody. All of Pitt's opponents knew about the new runner. They were watching films and hatching plots about how to stop him. At the same time, Tony was spending hours watching films of Northwestern's defense, so he'd know what to expect. If there was any weakness in the defense, the coaches pointed it out.

Northwestern University, in Evanston, Illinois, was a long way from Pittsburgh. As the game started and the wind blew a cold, hard rain in from Lake Michigan, it looked like it might be a long day and a long, long trip home. Pitt scored first, but Northwestern scored 14 points in the second quarter.

Tony was eating up the yards, a few at a time. In one drive, he gained 62 yards on eight carries. Then he fought the final six yards, and scored. At the half, the score was tied. Tony had gained 125 yards already, but it had taken him twenty-two carries to do it.

Something happened to the team during the half. Maybe they grew up. Maybe they started believing in themselves. Maybe it was just determination. But suddenly, everything started working right, like a big machine that's just had its wheels oiled.

The defense splashed down on Northwestern and held them scoreless. And Tony? Well, from his own 21-yard line, he broke off right tackle. He pushed off one tackler and steamed down field, skimming the field like a sea bird over water. Nobody got close to him. It was 79 yards, and a touchdown!

Pitt won the game 21–14. Tony had an unbelievable 265

Tony in action as a Pitt freshman. He autographed the picture to
Coach Ross: "To the man who got me started." (*Photo courtesy
Richard "Butch" Ross*)

yards rushing. That broke a Pitt record which had stood since 1930. The Pitt coaches didn't have to say anything to each other—their beaming faces showed what they now knew. In Tony Dorsett, they had one of the great ones!

Tony was just plain happy and excited. After the game, the players gave the game ball to Coach Majors for his first Pitt victory. Majors turned around and gave it to Tony. Tony deserved it, Majors said. Tony had shown everybody what he could do, and he'd done it under bad field conditions, too. It was a proud moment. It seemed like nothing could stop him now, unless it was Tulane. . . .

Tulane's Green Wave was dropping in on Pittsburgh Saturday. They were a big, fast team, and rated 15th in the country. And they'd be looking to get Tony Dorsett.

On Tony's first carry, he got up with only half a jersey left. In three carries, though, he gained 59 yards. Then he was thrown out of bounds, and he didn't get up.

Dorsett injured! A chill ran through the Pitt crowd. Tony's back and hip were badly bruised. But, after a rest, he went back in. He thought it would get better as he played.

But the pain kept getting worse. Tony, as Coach Ross would have told anybody, didn't want to leave the game. He just kept thinking, "I hope I can finish the game. I hope I can finish!"

Tony finished the game, but the team that had grown up the week before, fell apart today. Giving Tulane three pass interceptions and four fumbles, they lost 24–6.

Tony had gained only 77 yards, his worst game yet. He had a good excuse—his injury—but he didn't use it. He thought he should play well, no matter what else happened. And now the coaches were questioning whether he should play next week, against West Virginia.

But Tony was determined. Hurting or not, he was going to play against West Virginia.

TONY DORSETT

West Virginia University, in Morgantown, is only about 75 miles from Pitt. The two schools had been going against each other on cow pastures and football fields since 1895. And the fans had been going at each other in the streets for almost that long. It's the kind of local grudge game that sportswriters call a "backyard brawl," and sometimes the brawl extended to backyards and barrooms near the two stadiums.

At West Virginia, the saying is that they can lose every game, but if they beat Pitt they've had a winning season. At Pitt, losing to West Virginia is not just a disappointment, it's a disgrace.

No, Tony wasn't going to miss that game. Majors warned the team about the hostile crowd they'd find in Morgantown's Mountaineer Field. "Have poise for the noise," he told them in his unique style.

West Virginia's Mountaineer marching band didn't expect to help the Panthers, but then this was a year that anything could happen. The dust-up started when West Virginia did not allow Pitt to bring its band to the game. Mountaineer Field was too small, they said. They needed the Pitt band seats for their fans.

There was grumbling about that all week at Pitt. At game time, Majors sent the team charging out of the locker room, their adrenaline pumping. They ran into the tunnel . . . and stopped!

The players in the rear bumped into the ones in front. The Mountaineer band was standing in front of them, blocking the entrance.

The Panthers had to stand there and wait, watching the whitewash peel off the old concrete tunnel walls. As they waited, they could hear the crowd chanting, over and over:
"Pitt, Pitt, go back to the woods,
Your coach is a farmer,
And your team is no good!"

TONY DORSETT

By the time the Panthers listened to that for the twentieth time, they were ready to plow up the field with anybody. The Mountaineer band members were lucky. The Panthers didn't trample them, they just trampled the football team. The defense blitzed the Mountaineer quarterback and caught him for big losses.

Billy Daniels not only completed passes right and left, he faked one and scored the first Pitt touchdown. At the half, it was 14–0, Pitt!

Tony did his thing, too. He dazzled them with his magic feet. Cutting and weaving, he scored once from the 35. And scored twice more from the 12. He ran for 153 yards in all, and Pitt won, 35–7.

In the locker room after the game, Coach Majors tried to talk to reporters while his players poured soft drinks over his head. "Our players were sharp and crisp and had a lot of incentive out there today," he said.

An assistant coach said the same thing in another way. "They shouldn't have made us mad," he said.

CHAPTER IX

Back on the Pitt campus, people were starting to yell, "TD!" when they saw Tony going to class or eating in the cafeteria. His fellow students often asked for his autograph. And, once in a while, people were now seen wearing Panther T-shirts, and nobody thought they were weird any more.

The Panther team now had what Johnny Majors always called "pride and enthusiasm." It made a difference to the whole school. Membership in the Golden Panthers booster club was going up fast. Sports Information Director Dean Billick was getting more and more calls from all over the country for interviews with Johnny Majors, and with Tony Dorsett.

Tony was named to the United Press International (UPI) Backfield of the Week for the second time. Now he had to get up his nerve to face the national press. Getting calls from *Time* magazine or *Sports Illustrated* was a lot different than talking to reporters from the *Beaver County Times!*

Those New York reporters were enough to scare anybody, especially a shy nineteen-year-old kid from a small town. The first time Tony was interviewed on ABC-TV, he seemed cool. Only Jackie Sherrill saw what Tony was hoping nobody noticed—all the time he talked, his lips were quivering.

TONY DORSETT

The reporters discovered that they liked Tony. He gave them good, quotable quotes, he answered all their questions, and most of all he was sincere about it. Bill Hillgrove, the Pitt broadcaster, said, "One thing I always noticed about Tony from the very beginning was his sincerity. This came through when people would gather around him, and he would respond to exactly the question asked of him."

Hillgrove noticed Tony analyzing the reporters, just the way he analyzed plays on the football field. "When he saw that the pencils weren't moving on the papers, he would become more animated. He realized that, 'Okay, maybe I'm not saying enough.' He was that sensitive to what was going on around him."

Tony knew that if he kept doing well on the field, interviews would be part of his life, almost as much as football practice was. And he didn't let up in practicing for the next game, at Boston College. If the Back of the Week wouldn't let up, neither could the rest of the team, not when they saw him struggling into the back brace he'd had to wear since the Tulane game.

Because of the brace and a sore leg, Tony played decoy at Boston. He'd go one way, while somebody else with the ball went another. Even without carrying the ball as much, he still scored two touchdowns and rushed for 109 yards.

Pitt's defense, with Gary Burley back, let Boston College into Pitt territory only three times, as Pitt won 28–14.

Next was the big homecoming game against Navy, and it turned out to be another strange kind of game. Pitt won the first half, and Navy won the second . . . almost.

Only two minutes after the game started, Carson Long sent the Pitt fans into orbit by kicking a 47-yard field goal. It was the first Panther field goal in two years. After that, he kicked one of 30 yards, and then 49.

Meanwhile, Tony was running. He put his shoulder down and blasted through the line for 26 yards. Then he ran for

29 more. Finally, he went over the defensive line into the end zone.

The Pitt fans hardly had a chance to sit down. Carson Long's kicks had brought them to their feet. And something new was happening, too. Every time Tony got the ball and took more than a couple of steps, it seemed like a shock of electricity ran through the crowd. Tony was like a magnet—when he started to run, he pulled the crowd to its feet.

At the half, Pitt led 16–0. Waves of happiness were going up from Pitt Stadium, but they soon settled down into ripples of gloom. Navy scored a field goal, a touchdown, and then another touchdown. With only three minutes left to play, Navy tried a two-point conversion, and made it! Now Navy was leading 17–16!

Then Daniels and Dorsett got moving. From their own 33, Daniels passed and Tony ran, until they were on the 3-yard line with 33 seconds left in the game.

No matter what happened now, nobody was going to say that Pitt football wasn't exciting any more. One side of the hill leading up to Pitt Stadium is so steep that people call it "Cardiac Hill." Strong men have keeled over before reaching the top of it. But today, the fans were so excited they'd be more likely to fall over at the top and just roll all the way down!

They were on their feet, screaming. Thirty-three seconds! What would Majors do?

He sent Tony into the center of the line. He was stopped! But he didn't have the ball! Daniels had it, and he was running around right end. He was in the end zone! Pitt won 22–17!

As the heartbroken Middies trudged off the field, the Panther locker room started jumping. "How does it feel to finally get your first victory at home?" reporters asked. Gary Burley answered that for everybody. "It feels super," he said.

When Syracuse came into town the next week, the feeling was even better. Billy Daniels rushed for 165 yards and passed for another 121. All Tony did was rush for 211 as Pitt won 28–14.

Who is this kid—Superman? That's what people around the country were starting to wonder. Sure he is, said anybody in Pittsburgh.

But out in the Midwest, eleven guys were listening to all that talk. They weren't saying much, just clearing their throats, and laughing to themselves. Those eleven guys were the best rushing defense in the country at the time, and they were looking forward to coming to visit Tony Dorsett. They knew he was good, but they said they'd seen better. They planned to put him in his place, somewhere behind the line of scrimmage. Those eleven guys were, after all, the defense of none other than Notre Dame!

At Pitt, Majors was getting his team psyched up. They practiced against subs wearing green jerseys, ate Irish stew, and listened to the Notre Dame fight song blaring over the loudspeaker.

Majors used psychology in practice, too. He knew that Pitt was always losing to Notre Dame—and by big scores. Last year it was 42–16; the year before 57–7.

So, in going over the game plan, Majors and his assistants did not mention Notre Dame at first. They laid out Notre Dame plays on the blackboard, but they didn't call them Notre Dame plays. They called them Team X plays.

The coaches would say, suppose Team X did this . . . you do this, and you can stop them. After they had run through them on the field and felt confident that they really could stop those plays, Majors finally said, "If Team X runs that play, you know you can stop it. Now you know you can stop Notre Dame!"

Tony was watching Notre Dame films and figuring how to run outside on them. He and Ed Wilamowski, who was starting now at defensive end, hadn't forgotten their trip to Notre Dame. They wanted this game. Ed said, "Tony and I don't need any help to get fired up for Notre Dame!"

On game day, November 10, almost 57,000 people ignored the cold wind and spitting snow and filled Pitt Stadium. But they weren't all Pitt fans. Notre Dame has fans all over the country, and more people usually came to see Notre Dame than came to see Pitt.

Today, the Pitt crowd was bigger, and they were strung as tight as the band's bass drum. In the stands before the game there weren't any of the usual poker games, business meetings, fraternity elections—all those things Pitt fans used to do to keep their minds off the slaughter going on down on the field.

Today the Pitt fans were serious. Most people didn't expect to win, but they had hope. They thought they had a chance of seeing a real ball game here, at least. The chant went up before the game, and it kept up—"TD! TD! TD!"

Tony heard it, and it pleased him. He looked toward his mom and dad, who were always in the stands to watch him. He was determined, and he was ready for his biggest test.

Tony started running and running. He found holes and breezed through them. When the Irish closed the holes, he ran around the ends. But the Panthers' nervousness and lack of experience showed. On the Pitt 24, Daniels dropped a handoff to Tony. Notre Dame fell on it, and scored a few plays later.

The Panther defense knew they could stop Team X, but these Notre Dame linemen didn't look like Team X. They looked more like the Cathedral of Learning, on legs.

But, hey, when the Notre Dame offense got down to the Pitt 7-yard line, with first down and goal to go, the Panther defense stopped Team X! The Irish had to kick a field goal.

At the half, the score was 10–0. The Panthers thought

they still had a chance. "You're beating yourselves with mistakes," Majors told them in the locker room.

For the third quarter, Tony started from his own 14. He found a hole in the middle of the line. He whooshed past a surprised Irish linebacker and outraced everybody for 65 yards, skimming down the icy sideline until he was finally forced out of bounds on the 21.

After a field goal, the Panthers were soon coming back at the Irish again, with a 24-yard pass from Daniels to Bruce Murphy. Then Tony took off for 21 yards, to the 12-yard line.

The crowd wasn't getting cold today. They were jumping up and down every time Tony carried the ball. And they noticed something they thought was unusual. When Tony trotted back to the huddle, he was applauded—not only by the fans, but by his own teammates!

Dave Janasek dived over for a touchdown, and the score was 17–10. Pitt was close, but they couldn't get any closer. Slipping and sliding, they lost the ball seven times on fumbles or interceptions. As the game ended, Irish quarterback Tommy Clements, whose hometown was McKees Rocks, up the river from Aliquippa, passed for a touchdown, to make the final 31–10.

When the totals were added up, there was one that the Irish had trouble believing. Tony Dorsett had run, against the best defense in the country, for 209 yards!

Nobody else had ever gained that many yards against the Irish. And it looked to all the sportswriters like Tony Dorsett was going to be an All-American!

There were other people watching that game, too. They were men who hadn't been seen around the University of Pittsburgh in so many years that their presence caused an uproar. Those men were bowl scouts, and they were thinking about inviting Pitt to a post-season game. Their just

Tony shows a shifty move. (*Photo courtesy Sports Information Office, University of Pittsburgh*)

being there showed how far Pitt had come in only a year. And, oh boy, they liked that exciting freshman runner!

Bowl bids would come out the next week, but first the Panthers were looking forward to a trip to West Point. One Pittsburgh writer thought they might as well stay home. If the country had to depend on the Army football team to defend it, he wrote, we were all in trouble.

On a cold, windy field, Tony showed that writer knew what he was talking about. He ran for 100 yards in the first half, and 61 more before the first team was taken out of the game in the second half. He had a 42-yard run that set up a field goal, and did a neat somersault into the end zone for a TD.

After the 34–0 win, there was a ceremony at the Panthers' motel. The team put on Mexican hats, and Coach Majors and Athletic Director Cas Myslinski accepted an invitation to play against Arizona State in the Fiesta Bowl in Tempe, Arizona.

That would be on December 21, and Pitt's first bowl game since 1956 would be something to celebrate. But there was another game to play first. . . .

Well, not just another game. When Pitt plays Penn State, it's never just another game. The two big universities, about 3 hours' driving time apart, are what the newspapers always call "arch-rivals." If a Penn State fan said it was a nice day, a Pitt fan would deny it and find a cloud someplace to prove it.

If a Pitt fan said that Pitt would beat Penn State this year, the Penn State fan would laugh, and the fight would be on. But the Panthers did think they could win, this year. Tony was determined. The defense was determined. They wanted to prove they were as good as Penn State's famous defense.

The Pitt squad traveled by bus up to "Happy Valley," as Penn State's location in the mountains is nicknamed. Car and van loads of fans from both sides followed them from Pittsburgh.

At big Beaver Stadium, the Panthers were greeted by a heavy rainstorm. Looking like a battleship sitting out on the mountain, Beaver Stadium is an unfriendly place for outsiders, even in good weather. Penn State fans fight each other every year for tickets, and Pitt fans found themselves sitting in a ghetto at the corner of the end zone.

The rain stopped, but it left the field slippery. Tony started running well against Penn State's tough hitters, but he had to be careful not to slip and fall down, and that hurt his concentration.

In the second quarter, he broke two tackles and slanted 14 yards to score. Later, he took a hard tackle and limped off the field. The tackler exclaimed about how strong Tony's legs were: "Even when he's tackled, his legs don't stop moving!"

But Tony was soon back in the game and his 10-yard run put the Panthers in position for Carson Long to kick a field goal. It was a long one—for 50 yards, and it came as the clock ran out in the first half. Pitt led 13–3!

The Panthers jumped all over Long in celebration. The Penn State team watched. "The game's not over yet," they grumbled. And they came out fired up after the half.

Their defense held Tony to a game total of 77 yards—only the second game all year he'd had less than 100. Penn State scored once in the third quarter, and finally wore down the Pitt defense in the fourth. They scored twice more to win the game 35–13.

There was almost a month now to wait for the big trip to the Fiesta Bowl in Arizona. It was also a time when Tony should be hitting the books and getting ready for final exams. But he was exhausted and wasn't feeling well. He had worked so hard and been pounded so much that he was losing weight. He was down to 155 pounds and feeling weak. He talked about quitting again, but his mother and Coach Sherrill convinced him he'd be wrong to quit now, just when his career was starting to zoom.

With his record-breaking 1,586 yards rushing, he was named to all the All-American teams—the first freshman to do that since 1944!

There were banquets to go to, celebrations, speeches to make and, always, interviews to do. Tony's grades didn't always match his exploits on the field, but he squeaked through his first semester and practiced hard for the Fiesta Bowl at the same time.

Arizona State had an offense which seemed to explode like pinwheels and rockets in a fireworks display. They had averaged an unbelievable 49 points a game this year. Their team was stocked with future pro players like quarterback Danny White, fullback Ben Malone, and running back Woody Green. Green and Malone had rushed for more than 1,000 yards, each. And White had passed for 2,600. The Panther defense knew they'd be kept busy.

The Panthers drilled hard, but they had a good time in friendly Arizona, too. Coach Majors said that bowl games should be a reward for the players, and they rode horses, and saw the sights, and had a real vacation in the sun.

On the first play of the game, Pitt recovered a fumble on the Arizona 12. Tony swept around end for 8 yards. Then he ran 4 more for the touchdown! Only 47 seconds had gone by.

The Pitt defense was looking good, too. At the half, the score was tied, 7–7. But then Arizona State spread its defense out and stopped Tony's running outside. Both teams had fumbles, interceptions, and penalties, and Arizona State scored 18 points in the last quarter to win 28–7.

Majors comforted his tired players. "I'm disappointed, but

not embarrassed," he said. He was named Coach of the Year
by the Football Writers' Association. It was funny how often
Tony's coaches won that honor.

Tony's 100 yards rushing made him 1,686 for the year.
That, said Pitt officials, rubbing their fingernails and trying
to look modest, made him only the greatest freshman running back in major college history.

Tony always gave the credit for that to his teammates,
especially the offensive linemen. The trouble was, half the
offensive line was graduating.

And, over the summer, coaches at places like Notre Dame
and Penn State and—good grief!—Southern California, would
be making movies. They'd be splicing pieces of film together
to end up with "The Tony Dorsett Show." The film would
have clips of every time Tony ran the ball this year.

The coaches would watch that film until their eyeballs
were spinning. And then they would know how to stop
Tony Dorsett. They would have guards and tackles and
linebackers in all the right places, just waiting to bring
down the Hawk.

One thing worried them, though. Maybe it was the fault
of the film projector. Sometimes, when Tony started to run,
it looked like the film suddenly speeded up!

CHAPTER X

The Pitt coaches were pleased with themselves. They thought they were having a great recruiting year. Among outstanding prospects they'd signed were All-WPIAL tackle Tom Brzoza from New Castle; Randy Cozens, a junior college All-American; Karl Farmer, a world-class track sprinter, and Matt Cavanaugh, a quarterback with a rifle arm from Youngstown, Ohio, not far across the state line from Aliquippa.

Another recruit was running back Elliott Walker from Miami. He was the leading ground gainer in South Florida high school history.

Was Tony worried about a new running back beating him out? Of course reporters had to ask him that. "No," Tony said.

Reporters did like those honest answers of Tony's. Sometimes—like now—they sounded cocky. But Tony went on to explain to those who would listen that Walker was a different kind of runner. He was blockier than Tony, a power runner, and maybe they'd be a good combination together.

One of the best new recruits was Randy Holloway, who looked awesome at 6 foot 6, 215 pounds. He'd been All-WPIAL and All-State. He gave reporters his reasons for choosing Pitt. He said he wanted to get into a rebuilding program where he'd have a chance to play right away. He wanted to play near home so his family and friends could see him.

Those were two of the same reasons Tony had come to Pitt, but Randy had another one. He said he wanted to play with Tony Dorsett. That wasn't surprising, if you knew where Randy had played his high school ball. He had played for . . . the Sharon Bengals!

So Randy had seen Dorsett's revenge first hand. In the next three years, he might see it again, but it would be more fun to be on the same side!

Tony was thinking about next year, too. Once he'd made up his mind to play, he set a goal of gaining a thousand yards again. Another goal was also forming in the back of his mind. He was thinking about going into broadcasting some day. That might have seemed like a funny career for somebody as shy as Tony, but he was getting enough practice already to begin to believe that he could do it.

Watching all the reporters, Tony had been learning fast. He was getting the knack of sensing the kind of story each one wanted to write, and giving him that story. He could make each reporter feel he was getting an exclusive—a scoop—and the writers liked that.

Tony also learned how to give the same story to five or six different writers, but he'd tell it to each one in different words, so each one felt he had a different story.

While he was getting A's for good interviews, though, his professors were not that generous. Tony wasn't always working as hard in class as he knew he should be, and his grades at the end of the year showed that. They were good enough to allow him to stay in school, but they were not good enough to please Myrtle Dorsett!

She wanted him to do better—football wouldn't last forever. Tony knew that he needed his education, whether he decided to be a broadcaster or anything else, and he promised to study harder next year.

Knowing a tough year was coming up, Tony relaxed during the summer, doing odd jobs like mowing lawns. He kept running, though. Nobody dared report to training camp out of shape!

Tony and Ed were looking forward to the season, but not to training camp. Ed always said, "I can tell you when the hottest two weeks of the year are going to be—the weeks we're in training camp!"

Camp this year wouldn't be as confusing or as hectic as last year. Tony didn't have to prove anything to the coaches now, but he still couldn't let down. A few bad games could make people start saying he was washed up. One newspaper even predicted that Dorsett might turn out to be nothing but a "one-year flash!"

Coach Majors wasn't worried about Tony ever looking bad, nor the rest of the backfield, either. Bill Daniels was back at quarterback, Dave Janasek and his great blocking at fullback, and Bruce Murphy, who'd led the team in pass receiving last year at wingback. But then one by one, the whole backfield started getting injured. Most of the injuries weren't serious, but Tony had a painful groin pull. The team members weren't all able to practice at one time until a week before the first game.

Tony's weight pleased the coaches. He'd gained about 15 pounds over the summer, but it hadn't slowed him down. His body was just maturing, and his knowledge of the game was, too. But the coaches were worried about his injury, and so was Tony.

If he practiced more than an hour, his leg would start to stiffen up. He spent hours in the whirlpool bath and wore miles of tape, but it still bothered him. He admitted to Jeff Samuels of the *Pittsburgh Press* that, "I'm not really in as good shape as I was last year. I might get tired. I'll just go until I can't go any more."

He was concentrating on trying to be ready for the first game, at Florida State. It was supposed to be easy—a breather. The Florida State Seminoles had lost every game last year and the Panthers were favored to win by 19 points. Maybe it looked too easy, though.

The Panthers went down to Tallahassee with confidence. And almost lost it.

The Seminoles took the opening kickoff and marched for a touchdown. Then the Pitt offense couldn't get moving. Tony picked up some yards, but the Seminole defense was always there waiting for him. Five or six of them. This breather didn't seem like one. Breathing itself wasn't easy on this hot, humid Florida night. Running with only one good leg wasn't easy, either!

Tony had runs of 13, 13, and 6 yards to set up a field goal, but Long missed it. Just before the half ended, the Panthers recovered a Seminole fumble on the 17. Daniels passed to Murphy for 14 yards. Tony cracked through for two more. From the 1-yard line, Tony more or less sprouted wings and flew over the top to score.

With everybody missing kicks, it was 6–6 at the half. Only Carson Long's field goal in the third quarter saved the Panthers. The final score was 9–6. Tony was worn out with the heat and pain, and he had gained only 81 yards in twenty-one carries. That might be a great game for somebody else, but not making a hundred yards was a bad way to start the year for Tony. It gave the critics a chance to start wondering. "The offense needs a lot of work," wrote Ulish Carter in the *Pittsburgh Courier*. "As great as Dorsett is he can't be expected to do it all by himself."

Nobody on the offensive line expected Tony to do it all alone. They did know they were in for a rough time this year, with so much to learn and so little experience among them.

But Tony's leg was starting to feel better, and the team was feeling better with him as they flew south to play tough Georgia Tech. The field in Atlanta was more like an oven than anything else. If it wasn't a hundred degrees down there, it felt like it.

Down there in the trenches, with the pushing and shoving and sweating, and the "Oofs!" and "Ows!" and other words not so nice, any boy from Aliquippa might have wondered what advantage this occupation had over working at the open hearth furnace in the mill.

But by the time the steam had cleared in the fourth quarter, Tony had 168 yards and two touchdowns. After the game, he even got a few cheers from the Georgia Tech crowd when he took off his jersey and gave it to a little boy who ran over and asked him for it.

But he was tired. "The sun really takes it out of you in the second half," he said. The 27–7 win made the hard work seem worthwhile, but of course Georgia Tech was not exactly Southern California, whose Trojans were due to thunder into Pitt Stadium next week. The game was billed as a duel, between "TD East" and "TD West," better known as Tony Dorsett and Anthony Davis.

The two star runners had met during the summer in Chicago at an All-American dinner. Davis said he thought Tony looked like TV comic Flip Wilson, and that he knew a linebacker who would be glad to flip Tony any time. Tony grinned and mentioned somebody named Gary Burley who was anxious to return the favor to Mr. Davis.

But the kidding was over now. This was a game you'd call *big*. Fifty-five thousand people were coming to Pitt Stadium to celebrate the fiftieth year of football there in the old concrete oval with its shiny new aluminum seating and its artificial turf that sparkled in the sunshine. They also expected to celebrate Tony Dorsett's victory over Anthony Davis while they watched the Trojans go crying home to their mothers.

Well, some people expected that. Others were realists.

The Trojans not only had Davis, they had future-Los-Angeles-Rams quarterback Pat Haden and enough other future pro players to start their own franchise. No less than ten of them would soon do that, in fact. They would follow their coach, John McKay, to the new Tampa Bay Buccaneers.

The Trojans were in an ugly mood, too. They'd blown their first game, losing in an upset to Arkansas. That had just about killed their chances for the national championship they'd been supposed to win. They were out to get somebody now, and Pitt was in their road. It was like standing in the path of a runaway truck.

The young Panthers knew all that, and they couldn't help feeling nervous. But, early in the game, with the Trojans on the Pitt 6-yard line the defense threw Pat Haden back two yards. The Trojans had to kick a field goal.

To end the quarter, Pitt monster back Mike Bulino intercepted a pass on the Trojan 45. Then Tony cut through the middle and raced for 21 yards. He set up a touchdown, but he broke another record with that run too. Marshall Goldberg, Pitt's most famous runner, had rushed for 1,957 career yards back in 1936–38. Tony had now passed him with 1,964. He felt there was no limit to the records he could go on and break.

There wouldn't be any more records today, though, against the big Trojan line. But the Pitt defense wasn't out there to dance a ballet, either. In the second quarter, Randy Holloway and nose guard Al Romano stopped Pat Haden on a fourth and one on the Pitt 15. At the half, the score was Pitt, 7, Southern Cal 3.

TONY DORSETT

Pitt fans were hysterical. No matter what happened in the second half, many of them were already satisfied. Two years ago, if you'd told them they'd ever be leading Southern California at the half, they would have suggested you might have had a recent fall on your head which left you babbling nonsense!

In the second half, the Trojan offense controlled the ball for too long. The Panther defense was beginning to tire, and the offense couldn't get any long drives started. Tony carried only fifteen times, half as many as usual, and gained 59 yards. Anthony Davis had 149 yards, while the whole Pitt offense totaled only 99 yards.

The 16–7 score was closer than expected, but it was still a loss. The newspapers kept saying that Tony needed a better offensive line in front of him. But Tony never blamed the linemen. He knew he had to be patient. The freshmen and sophomores were getting better all the time.

Tony always thanked the linemen for good blocks and told them when they played well. He didn't make a big show of doing that on the field. He'd go over to one of them on the sideline and say quietly, "Good play," or just, "Thanks." They were as happy as he was when they could open a hole for him, and they loved watching Tony run. Sometimes they even forgot themselves and stopped just to watch him.

The next week, the offense did much better. They scored 29 points, playing against the Tar Heels in Chapel Hill, North Carolina.

That was the good news. The bad news was that the Tar Heels scored 45 points!

The game didn't start out badly. Tony took a pitchout and ran for 12 yards to start a long scoring drive. But then he went down—a sprained ankle. He missed seven plays. He went back in but the pain in his ankle kept him from making his best twists and cuts.

TONY DORSETT

On the sideline, the Tar Heel fans were laughing at what looked like a sewing circle around the Pitt bench. What?

Well, the shipment of Pitt's tearaway jerseys didn't come in time for the game. Tony and Bill Daniels had only three of them of the dozen or so they usually wore out in a game, so they were having to be sewn together between plays. The Pitt fans loved that, though. They claimed that Pitt had never even needed tearaway jerseys before Johnny Majors and Tony Dorsett showed up!

Tony gained only 59 yards in the game, and the defense was humiliated about giving up 45 points. "We just got a good old country tailwhipping," Coach Majors said.

On Sundays, the coaches always got up early to watch the game films and grade the players on how well they'd played the day before. The players dreaded hearing about those grades this week.

The fans and the sportswriters were all trying to analyze what was going wrong, too. Some said Tony was taking too much punishment on the field, running at those 270-pound linemen every week. "No," Tony said, "I don't run *at* them. I try to dodge them!"

Russ Franke of the *Pittsburgh Press* voiced the worry in the most colorful language: "For a meal ticket that gets punched 25 times every Saturday, it's a wonder to Pitt fans there is anything left of Tony Dorsett to punch!"

The Panthers themselves were more upset than anyone else. They got together for a team meeting. Everybody spoke up and talked about whatever was bothering him. Tony apologized for his performance. He said he thought he might be trying to read the defense too much, instead of just attacking. He admitted, "I'm not running as well as I did last year."

As Johnny Majors once analyzed the team, they were a "melting pot" of different types of people, and they had to learn to work together as a unit. Now they were getting with it. The team meeting helped clear the air, and it was a good thing it did. Next Saturday, the West Virginia Mountaineers were coming!

n the morning of the West Virginia game, Dave Janasek showed up with a bad foot infection. Majors asked sophomore Bobby Hutton if he was ready to start in Janasek's place.

"Yes, sir," Hutton said quickly. But on the way out of the room, Hutton looked around and whispered, "Whew! Was he serious?"

That was the way things were going for the Panthers this year. As soon as they thought they had everything together, something would fall apart again. Tony's leg still wasn't 100 percent, and with a new blocker the coaches were nervous about the offense.

But today Hutton came through. So did the rest of the offense. Tony gained 145 yards, and Pitt beat the Mountaineers 31–14. Now the Panthers were rolling again!

The next week Tony felt ready to break a long run. He hadn't really done that all year, and it was building up inside him like a time bomb ready to explode.

Boston College was unlucky enough to be the team on the field when the time bomb went off. Pitt was ahead 14–3 in the third quarter. Tony broke through the line and then whirled completely around. The Boston secondary came in close. They thought Tony had been stopped. He hadn't.

TONY DORSETT

With the fans on their feet screaming, "TD! TD!" Tony streaked down the field—61 yards for a touchdown. Back on the 42-yard line was a piece of his jersey. And on the 37 was another piece of it. Almost shirtless, Tony was mobbed by his teammates at the goal line. Wow! It felt good to break loose like that at last.

The fans enjoyed that run almost as much as Tony did. Most people have dreamed sometimes about being able to take off and fly through the air, and watching Tony gave them a feeling of what that must be like.

The feeling was even stronger for Tony. He thought he'd like to do that again before the day was over. So he did.

Willie Taylor and John Takacs help Tony celebrate a touchdown. (*Photo courtesy Sports Information Office, University of Pittsburgh*)

This time it was 74 yards, straight up the middle. And nobody even touched his jersey. He had three touchdowns and 191 yards in only fourteen carries, and Pitt won 35–11.

At Navy the next week, the game was as heart-stopping as last year's. On Pitt's first series of plays, Tony limped off the field, sending shock waves back to Pittsburgh so strong they could almost be picked up on radar.

But Tony wouldn't stay down. After the trainers worked on his right knee, he ran back into the game, to pick up 108 yards in twenty-five carries.

In the fourth quarter, with the score 6–3 on Long's two field goals, Pitt was finally on the Navy seven. But it was fourth down and a yard to go. Would Majors call for a field goal?

No! He gambled. And they got the first down. Then Tony barreled over the line for two yards to score. Navy came came back, with a minute to go, and scored, too. They added a two-point conversion. It was 13–11, Pitt.

In Pittsburgh, people were crowded around their radios. They were biting their nails and pounding on the radio, the table, or each other. They knew an on-side kick was coming. So did everybody in the stadium in Annapolis.

In the spirit of, "Don't give up the ship," Navy tried the short kick . . . and recovered it.

Now everything depended on the Panther defense. They held. Navy had to give up the ball just as the game ended, still 13–11.

Tony left Annapolis with his leg hurting. But he'd be back in two years, and his return would make headlines in more places than Pittsburgh!

Now Tony had to get ready for a trip to Syracuse, New York. Old Archbold Stadium there was filled with long grass and, some people claimed, gopher holes. Running in long grass didn't bother somebody who'd learned to run around stones and through the weeds on an Aliquippa hillside.

But it could slow him down just a little, and Tony always had his best games on artificial turf.

On Pitt's first drive, Tony carried the ball eight times for 35 yards. Then he took a pitchout from Daniels to score from the one. But Syracuse came back, and led 10–7 at the half.

In the third quarter the Panthers started a long drive from their own 5-yard line. Daniels' passing took them to midfield, then Tony took another pitchout and fought his way for 12 yards.

He was hit hard and had to be helped off the field. The trainers thought he had re-sprained his ankle. As he sat with ice on his leg, trying to pretend it didn't hurt, he had to watch his teammates score a touchdown without him. Nobody knew how much he hated not being in there, but he was as happy as anybody when they scored.

Syracuse threatened until the final minute of the game, to give the Pitt fans another hair-raising finish. But Pitt won 21–13.

The Panthers had been struggling, but now they had a record of six wins and two losses. At least they would end up with a winning season. All they had left to do was to beat Temple, one of the better teams in the East, and, then, Notre Dame and Penn State. Panther fans would plan the defeat of those two with great confidence. Then they would look toward the sky, hoping they wouldn't be struck by lightning.

Temple was hoping lightning would strike in Pitt Stadium —their coach bragged that he had *two* Tony Dorsetts in his backfield. And on game day, Pitt didn't even have one Tony Dorsett!

Tony's injury had kept him out of practice all week, and the coaches decided not to let him play. "He could have played," said assistant coach Bob Matey, with fierce admiration. "Tony could play with anything!"

But the coaches didn't want to risk a further injury. It would be better to rest him so he'd be ready for Notre Dame.

The Homecoming crowd was disappointed at not seeing Tony play, but not as disappointed as Tony was. Elliott Walker, who had been playing at both tailback and fullback, now showed what he could do, and that was to score four touchdowns as Pitt won 35–24.

Tony was happy for Elliott. He wasn't jealous, but he did hate to see somebody else doing his job. He knew he'd be ready for Notre Dame next week.

Tony didn't practice much the first of the week, but the last two days showed he was able to start again. Ed Wilamowski had been bothered with injuries, too, but the two were willing to play Notre Dame on crutches, if they had to.

Even Notre Dame wasn't above hearing the charge of letting their stadium grass grow extra long or, well, not trimming it as short as usual, to slow Tony down. Whether or not the grass was long, it was wet. The fanatic Notre Dame fans didn't mind sitting in the rain, but the field was too slippery for Tony to get his good runs outside.

The Irish shocked the Panthers by driving down the field and scoring on their first possession. After that, both defenses kept the offense away from the goal. Then Hopewell High showed up. Pitt blocked a Notre Dame punt, and Ed recovered it on the Irish 12.

Tony and Bruce Murphy got the ball down to the 1-yard line. But Tony . . . oh! . . . fumbled it away. He almost wished he could die, right there.

Tony always said that in football you have to forget what's past and go on. This time, doing that was harder than ever. It looked like the Irish were going to take that fumble and make a score out of it. They drove down to the Pitt 10, and then *they* fumbled it away!

TONY DORSETT

Later, Pitt intercepted a pass on the Irish 44, and Tony tried something he hadn't been seen doing much since high school. He took a pitchout from Daniels and dropped back. Then he threw a pass to Daniels.

But Daniels was hit so hard he dropped the ball and had to leave the game. Bob Medwid filled in. He was a senior who'd been out with a bad knee for two years. He was from McKees Rocks, the same town as Irish quarterback Tommy Clements. Daniels was from Coraopolis, down the river from McKees Rocks, on the way to Aliquippa. There were enough of the Ohio River-Beaver Valley boys on the field to have a neighborhood reunion. But not today. It wasn't all that friendly out there.

Medwid passed the ball down the field for a touchdown and Pitt took the lead 10–7. It wasn't till the last quarter that Notre Dame scored again to go ahead 14–10. On the last play of the game a Medwid pass arched into the end zone, and fell . . . incomplete.

Pitt was so close, but not close enough . . . not yet. Tony had gained only 61 yards, but he said he'd be back. If the Irish fans didn't know what he meant, fans of the Sharon Bengals knew.

After Notre Dame, the Panthers were glad to have more than a week to nurse their bruises before the big annual head-basher with Penn State. This game would be played on Thanksgiving night and carried on national TV. Since Pitt Stadium did not have lights, the game had been moved to Three Rivers Stadium, the big new home of the Pittsburgh Pirates and Steelers, who were on their way to their first Super Bowl this year.

It was exciting to dress in the same locker rooms and play on the same field as the big pro teams, and the Panthers were full of hope. For almost the first time all year, their whole backfield was healthy. Majors said the offensive line was now playing better than they had in two years, and the defense had improved, too. Tony and the whole team were anxious to get at those Nittany Lions and their big reputation as the best team in the East.

On the night before the game, the Panthers had a quiet Thanksgiving dinner together. Pitt and Penn State alumni all over the country were making plans to finish off their turkeys early so they could get to the TV and watch their favorite team stuff the other one.

In Pittsburgh, as many fans as could beg, borrow, or scalp tickets crowded into the stadium, prepared to freeze for the team. Three Rivers Stadium stands at the point where the Monongahela and Allegheny Rivers join to form the Ohio. In November, it's an icebox. Fans near the top of the stadium huddled in blankets and hoped the wind wouldn't catch them and blow them down the Ohio.

Cold as they were, the fans weren't wishing they'd stayed home and watched the game on TV. The Lions had two field goals, but Medwid was hitting his receivers with short passes. Then Tony slashed through for two yards and a touchdown.

At the half, Pitt was leading 7–6. The Penn State half of the crowd was grouchy. They were seeing something they didn't like—Pitt fans, looking happy!

Lion coach Joe Paterno wasn't happy. In spite of the freezing weather, he had thrown off his coat during the first half. He said he was hot under the collar.

Paterno's teams always hit hard, and Tony was feeling the effects. Coach Paterno trained his defense not to run *to* the ball carrier, but *through* him. He also told them to gang-tackle the runners, to demoralize them.

Tony wasn't demoralized, but he felt like he'd been run through a few times. Those big Penn State tacklers seemed to be in the Pitt backfield as much as he was.

In the second half, the Lions opened up their passing game, too. By the time the game ended, the Panthers might not have been demoralized but they were beaten 31–10.

Tony was held to 65 yards, but that was enough to put him over 1,000 again for the year, with 1,004. He had slipped a little in national standing, and was named to the All-American second team. It had been a rough season, painful both mentally and physically and, in the end, disappointing. The Panthers had hoped for another bowl game this year, but the bowl scouts passed them by.

Well, next year would be better, they all said. Right now, Tony had to get to his books. Final exams were coming up, and yards rushing didn't count on one of those.

Slowly, Tony's grades were improving. And, after a rest, he had to get back into a weight-lifting program. Although he had always been strong, this would help him brush off and survive hits by those big tacklers who weighed almost twice as much as he did.

Tony not only worked on his neck and shoulder muscles, he built up his thigh muscles, too. Done in the right way, with the weight coach supervising, that wouldn't slow him down. It could give him more power and quickness than ever.

Coach Harry Jones looked at Tony's muscles and said, "He's so tight you couldn't pinch him with a pair of tweezers!"

An Oklahoma native who had been an All-American running back himself, at Arkansas, Jones always said things in a colorful way. When asked to describe Tony's running, he said, "He's quick as a hiccup and tough as week-old bread!"

In private, the coaches called Tony something else. They called him "the franchise."

CHAPTER XII

One day in practice, "the franchise" went down. He was knocked out. The players and coaches near him froze.

As if they were being pulled by wires, their heads all turned in the same direction—toward Johnny Majors. He was at the far end of the field and hadn't seen what happened. But he sensed the panic coming down the field at him. He started jogging toward it. Then he ran faster.

By the time he reached Tony, he was coming on a dead run. In those few seconds, the trainers had also reached Tony and were bringing him around. He was all right. The frozen statues took a breath again.

What a scare! Every man on the field knew how important Tony was to this team. And this year Majors was putting in a new offensive system he hoped would make even better use of Tony's talents. The new offense was called the Veer. Majors thought it fit his speedy backfield better than the I-formation.

Besides Tony, who ran 40 yards in 4.4 seconds (and some people claimed it was really 4.3), Elliott Walker ran a 4.4. Bobby Hutton was no slowpoke at 4.6.

At quarterback, junior Bob Haygood looked as if he would be the starter. He had 4.5 speed and had been great on punt returns the past two years. Sophomore Matt Cavanaugh was coming up, too, and was fighting for the job. He was a little slower than Haygood, but he was a good passer.

In the new formation, Tony would line up almost beside the quarterback instead of behind him, 4½ feet behind the line. As quick as he was, he could be through the defensive line from there, almost before they saw him.

Being closer to the line, he'd have less time to look for holes in it. The coaches weren't too worried about that. They knew the Hawk's eyes were even faster than his feet.

The Veer might also keep the defenses from concentrating so much on Tony. With Walker lining up on the other side of the quarterback, they'd have to watch both sides, not just try to figure out where Tony was going.

On defense, Gary Burley was gone to the Cincinnati Bengals, and only two starters were back in the offensive line. With two new quarterbacks and a new offense, Majors was worried about them making too many mistakes.

Tony didn't act worried. He smiled and said, "The Hawk is going to fly high again!"

In August, his weight was up to 180 pounds, and he was anxious for the season to start. Training camp was the usual struggle to produce what Majors called "superb conditioning."

Superb conditioning meant one thing—hard work. Or, as one player described training camp, "Think of the worst time you ever had in your life, and stretch it out over two weeks!" Johnny Majors always said that football should be fun, but training camp didn't count.

Added to the "fun" at camp this year was the drill, drill, drilling in the new Veer formation. In the Veer, the quarterback had four options—four different types of plays he could use. When he got the snap from center, he looked at the defensive tackle to see which way he was going. If the tackle was moving to the outside, the quarterback could hand the ball off to a halfback, who would drive between the tackle and guard.

If the tackle was coming inside, the quarterback slid down to the end of the line. If the defensive end was coming for him, he could give the ball to his other halfback, who was trailing and going farther outside. If the end was taking the halfback, the quarterback could either run the ball himself or fake to the halfback, then drop back and pass to the tight end.

Whatever he did, he had only seconds to decide. No wonder Majors was worried. In the first game, against the Georgia Bulldogs, he'd be trying this new system with two quarterbacks who had never started a game!

In hot and humid Athens, Georgia, the Veer began to look like an overheated engine—one that wouldn't run. Tony gained only 17 yards in the first half. Pitt trailed 7–0.

In the third quarter, Carson Long kicked two field goals. The quarter was almost over before Tony finally got loose for 27 yards. The Panthers now had to make two touchdowns before they got six points. Walker scored first on a pitchout, but a penalty put the ball back on the 20-yard line.

The Panthers had to try again. Tony caught a pass for 10 yards, then Haygood and Walker dived the rest of the way. When Haygood tried to run for a 2-point conversion, he was stopped.

Now it started to rain. The players' helmets looked like tea kettles pouring off steam.

Pitt finally started a long drive that took 7 minutes and ended with a touchdown. After hitting up the middle for a couple of first downs, Tony broke two tackles and started running. He was at the Georgia 18 before he was stopped. Soon, Haygood scored. Pitt won the game 19–9, and Tony had 104 yards.

TONY DORSETT

It was a happy ride home that night, except for certain questions reporters kept asking. Those questions were about the Oklahoma Sooners, who were looming ahead of the Panthers like giant shadows on the wall. They were ranked Number 1 in the country, and the Panthers had to go out to Norman, Oklahoma, to play them before 70,000 rabid fans. The Sooners had eight All-Americans and a 20-game winning streak.

Johnny Majors didn't show any doubts as he headed west with his team, but then neither did General Custer.

The Panthers did better than Custer's men—they got out of the massacre alive. Tony had the worst game he'd played since Sharon—17 yards rushing. The final casualty report was Oklahoma 46, Pitt 10.

Tony tried to keep a good attitude about the wipe-out. He told a press luncheon later, "I forgot about it right after it happened. It wasn't something you'd want to remember."

Later he would say, "As far as I was concerned, there were eight or nine games left, and I felt I had to redeem myself. I knew I was a better athlete than that 17-yard game showed. No, it wasn't that I had to show people, I felt I had to prove it to myself."

The whole team wanted to prove something now. This week, somebody else was going to be massacred. As the William and Mary College Indians trotted into Pitt Stadium they knew they had been chosen to be the victims.

The Panther defense stopped the Indians for no gain so many times they thought they must be facing the U.S. Cavalry. Tony started slowly, with 15 yards in six carries. Then he got on his horse, or seemed to. The Hopewell combination got together again as Ed recovered a fumble and Tony carried it over in a few plays to score.

When the war dance was over, Tony had 142 yards and three touchdowns. Carson Long had four field goals. Two new receivers, Gordon Jones and Willie Taylor, had shown they could catch the ball upside down, sideways, horizontally, and every other way but wrong.

The 47–0 score showed what the Panthers could do when they got everything together. It gave them back the confidence they needed after Oklahoma.

Against Duke the next week, the Panthers came up against a tougher defense. The game was a defensive battle, the kind that fans sometimes call boring.

Those games aren't boring to the players, though. Breaking a long run was the most exciting thing for Tony, but there was plenty of challenge and satisfaction in fighting for a yard or two. His coaches all talked about how Tony's quick starts and strong legs could make 2 or 3 or 4 yards at times when anybody else would have been stopped for a loss.

The Panther defense held Duke to 33 yards rushing, but Tony was held to 84 yards. After a long day butting heads and scraping elbows on the scratchy turf, the Panthers came out ahead 14–0.

Coming up next was a breather—they hoped—against the Temple Owls. The fans in Philadelphia must have known what was coming, because only 10,000 of them showed up. The Pitt fans who made the trip enjoyed themselves.

Every Pitt player was a star that day. Cornerback J. C. Wilson not only intercepted two passes, he recovered two fumbles and returned a blocked field goal 52 yards for a TD.

Gordon Jones caught a 75-yard pass from Haygood. Carson Long kicked two field goals and seven extra points. Tony rushed for 114 yards and caught two passes for 80. The defense was all over the ball, and the score ended Pitt 55, Temple 6.

After winning a high-scoring game, it was natural that the players wanted to kid around, take it a little easy in practice. But Coach Majors wouldn't have any of that. The Panthers reported on Sunday as usual to practice without pads. During the week, their schedule was the same as always—watching films from one o'clock to four, practice till six.

After dinner, it was back to the films until after eight o'clock. Tuesdays and Thursdays the players were due in the weight room for workouts whenever they could fit them into their class schedules. They didn't have a choice about whether or not to work out, just when.

Next week they had to go up to West Point, where Army was looking tougher than Temple. On Friday, a miserable rain greeted the Pitt team and the big group of fans and Golden Panther boosters. It looked like the whole East Coast was going to be fogged in. The big question talked about in hotels that night was whether Tony would be able to run in weather like this.

On Saturday morning, just before the game, the rain suddenly stopped. The visiting Pitt fans nodded their heads. Maybe this was a good omen. But Tony was still worried about the field. It was soaked and he thought he might not be able to get his footing.

When he tried to accelerate the first time, he found the ground wasn't as slippery as he thought. He, and Walker and Haygood, started making good yardage. On their first drive, Walker scored. On the second, the Panthers wrestled their way to the Army 17. Tony whooshed through the middle for 10 yards. But then he lost the ball! Army recovered.

How Tony hated that! As he trudged off the field, linebacker Arnie Weatherington gave him a pat. "Do a jog," Arnie said. "We'll get the ball back for you, and you can go all the way next time."

Tony picked right up on that. Such a prediction always turned him on. He loved to make it come true. Nobody knew how he did it, but he seemed to have the knack for making it come true in the most dramatic way.

And in the next minute, safety Dennis Moorhead intercepted an Army pass, and Tony was weaving and dancing his way for a 14-yard touchdown!

With runs of 66, 21, and 35 yards, he scored three more touchdowns. The Pitt fans were pounding each other and screaming, "Put the *Russian* army in! Tony'll run over them, too!"

By the end of the half, Tony had 218 yards. Majors took the first team out in the third quarter, when Tony had gained 268! Tony was now Pitt's all-time top scorer, and the Army was down 52–20. What a day!

But (in football, there's always a "but" coming along to worry you) Pitt's next opponent was Navy. Navy had just lost to lightweight Boston College, and they might be extra mean this week. Coach Majors was one who refused to underrate the Navy team. At a press luncheon, he warned that Navy would be tough—remember last year?

But the reporters didn't want to hear about last year. They wanted to hear about Tony Dorsett. Majors didn't mind talking about his favorite subject. "The last two games he's run better than he ever ran before," he said, "and I know it's going to continue. He has the legs to run like that and the heart to back up the legs."

Majors had brought Tony to the luncheon with him and he came out with some of his quotable quotes, on the Veer formation: "At first I liked the I-formation more, but I'm getting to like the Veer now. I think that it's only natural that an athlete who's had some success doesn't like to change.

"The Veer makes you a better back," Tony said. "You have to read more, because it sets up so close to the line."

Everybody enjoyed the lunch. Every football fan in Pittsburgh was happy. Attendance at Pitt games had already doubled since Majors and Dorsett had started putting on their shows, and 40,000 jolly people came to see Pitt sink the Navy.

TONY DORSETT

On the first play, Tony broke through the line and looked like he was going all the way. But a linebacker put out a hand and just managed to trip him, after 19 yards. When Gordon Jones returned a punt 52 yards to the Navy 15, Tony fumbled on the next play. On another long drive, he fumbled again. Then Haygood fumbled. And a pass was intercepted.

When a few things started going wrong, everything went wrong. The harder the Panthers tried, the worse it got. In the fourth quarter, it was 17–0, *Navy*. Tony heard something that shocked him. The jolly crowd had turned hostile. Some of the Pitt fans were booing!

That was awful for Tony. He tried not to hear, but he couldn't help it. It hurt.

The fans weren't booing Tony. They weren't booing anybody in particular. They were just frustrated. They wanted the Panthers to throw more passes. They wanted to see Tony break one. They wanted to see a win.

They didn't want to see fumbles, and they didn't want to see Navy score. But that's what they were seeing.

Late in the fourth quarter, it looked like Pitt was finally going to get a touchdown. The Panthers had the ball on the Navy 7, with first down and goal to go. But on fourth down Haygood was stopped short of the goal.

Tony took the blame on himself. He told reporter Jeff Samuels about being tackled at the 2-yard line. "I didn't fall forward. You always try to fall forward and I didn't. I could've had a touchdown. That's the price you pay."

"I think we took them lightly," he added. "It was a mental letdown. They just went out there and took it to us instead of us taking it to them."

An unhappy week of practice followed that game. But Majors didn't want his players unhappy. He wanted them angry. He wanted them to play with "angry poise." In other words—no mistakes this time.

Then there was more bad news. Haygood had an injured hip and wouldn't be able to play this week against Syracuse. Matt Cavanaugh would get his first start. He was still a question mark.

There were other question marks, too. Could the Panthers come back from that lifeless showing against Navy? Could they eliminate their mistakes? And could they do it with a new quarterback?

CHAPTER XIII

Pitt is on the Syracuse 22-yard line. Tony Dorsett takes the ball. He drops it! Syracuse recovers!"

Pitt fans turned off their radios. They didn't want to hear the rest. They were sorry later.

Pitt's next drive took only six plays to score. Cavanaugh was hitting his receivers on long passes, and Tony was hitting the long grass like he owned it.

The Panthers scored again, then, from his own 27, Tony took a pitchout left. He cut through the middle of the line, and then turned on the steam. He ran 73 yards for a touchdown!

Seeing Tony go like that was a great feeling for the linemen. They always blocked their men at the line of scrimmage and then ran downfield to block the secondary, too. They loved it when, every few plays, Tony came breezing by. With him around, they knew their extra efforts would pay off sooner or later.

That day gave all the Panthers a great feeling. They won the game 38–0, and Tony ran for 158 yards to go over the 1,000-yard mark for the third year. If he could do it again next year, he'd do something no college runner had ever done—rush for 1,000 yards in each of four seasons.

After Syracuse, the Panthers had to be ready to go to

Morgantown, West Virginia—that friendly city which turns vicious and starts foaming at the mouth once every two years. That happens when the Pitt Panthers come to town.

Mountaineer Field sat on a hillside above the Monongahela River, which flowed on north to Pittsburgh. Trotting into that stadium was like going into a snake pit. In fact, that's what the Pitt players called the field. But a Pitt fan who said that too loudly might find himself traveling back home by way of the river, and without a boat.

Mountaineer Field was packed, and more crowds were sitting on the roofs of buildings overlooking the upper side of the stadium. West Virginia's Mountaineer mascot sent a jolt through the Pitt players by firing off his rifle. But that was about the loudest noise heard through the first half as the game settled into a defensive battle. Pitt was trying to do what the sportscasters call "establish their running game" and didn't throw a pass in the whole first quarter.

By the end of the half, they had only three first downs. They hadn't come near the goal line, but neither had the Mountaineers. Fans on both sides were heard yawning loudly.

After the half, a different game started. First West Virginia scored. Matt Cavanaugh fired a 28-yard pass to Gordon Jones for a Pitt score. But then West Virginia scored again. Late in the fourth quarter, Cavanaugh passed for 9 yards to Tony for another TD.

Now it was 14–14, and the fans were awake. In fact they were going crazy. In that stadium, the seats are up close to the field. Mountaineer fans threw ice from paper cups down on the Pitt bench. The screaming and the tension and the tie score and the seconds ticking away rapidly on the clock were starting to rattle both teams. The game had turned into a thriller.

It wasn't over yet, either.

The Mountaineers punted. Then Tony broke two tackles

and got away for 22 yards to the West Virginia 28. But Pitt was penalized for clipping and was sent back to the 49.

Cavanaugh's pass was intercepted, and the noise almost sent the stadium sliding down the hill toward the river.

The Mountaineers started moving, all the way to the Pitt 17. Then they fumbled! The Panthers had their last chance.

They tried to get downfield in a hurry. But they couldn't do it. The sideline marker said third down. The Panthers were setting up for a pass. Cavanaugh was going to try to pass out of bounds to stop the clock and gain more time.

Wait a minute! The Panthers looked up to see their offensive coach, Joe Avezzano, running out on the field. He wasn't allowed to do that!

The Panthers watched him in shock until they finally heard what he was yelling. "Kick! Kick! It's *fourth* down!" Oh, no!

The players looked at the scoreboard clock. It did say fourth down. And *now* the sideline marker said fourth down, too. If Cavanaugh's pass had been incomplete, the Mountaineers would have had the ball on the Pitt 25, with 20 seconds left—maybe enough time to score.

The Panthers were in a real mess now. They were penalized back to their own 12-yard line for unsportsmanlike conduct and delay of game. Larry Swider punted out to the Pitt 48, but then Mountaineer quarterback Dan Kendra passed for 26 yards down the sideline and the receiver ran out of bounds. The clock stopped. There were four seconds left. It was time enough to try a field goal. The stadium seemed to be rocking like a boat.

Onto the field ran Mountaineer kicker Bill McKenzie. He was a walk-on, meaning that he hadn't been recruited and didn't even have a football scholarship. He could be a hero here, or he could miss the kick and maybe have to change his name and move to Australia.

For McKenzie, this was like a moment in a dream—the

kind of dream where you are meeting the President of the United States and suddenly look down and see that you are wearing only your pajamas!

McKenzie was shaking. He felt numb all over. He wasn't the only one—the Panthers were still in shock.

The clock started. McKenzie kicked the ball and kept his head down. He couldn't force himself to look. He didn't know what had happened till half the Mountaineer crowd swarmed out of the stands and knocked him over. It took a while for him to realize that the crowd was mobbing him to congratulate him, not to hang him!

The Panthers were stunned. There was nothing to do but get out of town as fast as they could and leave the celebrating to go on all night in Morgantown. Tony had ended up with 112 yards but, like all the Panthers, he was hurting.

The hurt was more mental than physical today. But after any game, Tony's back could look like he had been clawed by wild animals. With so many tacklers grabbing at him, their fingernails left their marks. He often had deep cuts and scratches, and even the shoulder pads could cut. Artificial turf always made brush burns, and bruises were a way of life. And those were the days the papers said he had no injuries!

Tony was used to all that. But this wild finish took a while to sink in. Coach Majors couldn't think of anything very cheerful to say, for once. "We didn't play well enough to win, but we didn't play bad enough to lose," was the best he could come up with for the press.

He wanted to put the West Virginia nightmares behind him and out of the players' minds. He had to, because there was another possible nightmare coming up next Saturday.

The Irish of Notre Dame had not forgiven Tony for making them look bad two years ago by gaining 209 yards. That was embarrassing, and Notre Dame did not like being embarrassed.

Tony also knew that he had to get West Virginia out of his mind. He ran after practice and stayed late studying Notre Dame films. Everybody did. Majors threw up his hands and said, "All I can do now is stay up a little later and get up a little earlier!"

On Saturday, the Irish took possession of the Pitt Stadium turf with all the confidence of the champions they knew they were. Their crew of All-Americans and future pros looked big, fast, and mean.

The Panthers came out shaky and disaster prone, with fear in their eyes. Well, that's how they were supposed to be. But these trembling, nervous Notre Dame rejects took the football. And in one minute they scored seven points!

How did they do that? Too-small Tony Dorsett first ran wide for 14 yards. Then he ran long for 57. He was forced out of bounds at the 3, but Cavanaugh scored from there.

The 56,000 people who packed Pitt Stadium never sat down. If they had come to relax, they were in the wrong place.

Notre Dame came right back with a field goal. Then Pitt fumbled the kickoff at the goal line. Uh-oh. Disaster time again. The Irish turned that into a touchdown.

Now it was 10–7, Notre Dame. Tony Dorsett had had enough of disasters. He took a pitchout from Cavanaugh and yanked away from a tackler. A small tornado blurred along the sideline. It was Tony. He went 71 yards for another TD!

Fans looked at the scoreboard and shook their watches. They couldn't believe it was still the first quarter. TD had carried the ball only four times, and he had 151 yards!

The Irish defenders were shaken now, and angry. Every time they looked up, Tony was behind them. Stopping him today was like trying to build a dam on the Monongahela with toothpicks. And, like the Monongahela, Tony just kept pouring through.

Tony runs away from a tackle. (*Photo courtesy Sports Information Office, University of Pittsburgh*)

TONY DORSETT

Today, the nightmares belonged to the Irish. By the time they woke up, Tony Dorsett had run against them for 303 yards!

Pitt had not only beaten the Irish 34–20, for the first win since 1963, but Tony had wiped them out. Hey, he showed them he was big enough!

After the game, the locker room was a madhouse. The Panthers accepted a bid to play against Kansas in the Sun Bowl in El Paso, Texas. Tony was mobbed by reporters who wanted to talk about something they never expected to see in their lifetimes—a 303–yard game against Notre Dame? "Did you think you could do that, Tony?"

Tony answered patiently. Suddenly, he said, "Excuse me." He went over to talk to a young boy who had been watching quietly.

The reporters had to figure that one out. When they did they found out something about Tony that not many people knew. The boy was suffering from leukemia, and Tony had been visiting him in the hospital.

Without publicity, he had been spending many hours at Children's Hospital, down the street from Pitt Stadium. On Saturdays the sick children could hear the cheering at the stadium and it was the thrill of a lifetime for them when Tony came bouncing into their rooms. He liked to kid around with them and encourage them. Somehow, he could make them feel they were going to be all right. Tony had a special feeling for those kids. Even on his biggest day in football, he had time to talk to his young friend who was very ill.

Outside the stadium, Pitt fans were stumbling down the hill, happily reliving the game. They knew that now Pitt was going to beat Penn State.

The big game was on national TV again, the Saturday after Thanksgiving. It was the usual freezing November night. Even before the game started, the fans who crowded into Three Rivers Stadium were complaining about their feet being numb with the cold. That might have been a bad sign. Numb feet were almost a symbol for this game.

As expected, the game was a grinding battle fought out like World War I, between the foot soldiers in the trenches. No big gains were made until the second quarter. From the Penn State 37-yard line, Tony took off around the end. A Penn State linebacker raced after him. While Tony was being tackled, Elliott Walker was racing through the hole left by the linebacker. And he had the ball!

Walker went the whole 37 yards for a Pitt TD. As Carson Long prepared to kick the extra point, Pitt fans smiled confidently. Carson had kicked 60 straight extra points, without missing. Of course, his wife had had a baby just a few hours before, and he might be a little shaky, but that surely wouldn't throw his aim off.

What Pitt didn't know was that Penn State had a secret plot. When the Lion coaches were watching Pitt films to prepare for the game, they noticed that on kicks, just before the snap, the Pitt center was dropping his head and bending his elbows. The Penn State coaches thought if they could get a man to jump over that center as soon as his head went down, it would give him an extra second, and he might block the kick.

Tom Odell was the lucky Penn State player chosen to commit suicide on the play. He practiced it all week. Now was the time. The whistle blew, the center dropped his head and raised his elbows, and Odell went head first over the top.

It worked! The kick was blocked. Odell was battered and bruised, but Pitt led by six points instead of seven.

Penn State didn't score until the fourth quarter. Now the Panthers were behind 7–6, and that blocked kick was looking very big. With a minute and a half left in the game, the Panthers set up a field goal. Carson had already missed one, but it was a 51-yarder, and anybody could miss from that distance. This one would be only 23 yards—a sure thing. It wasn't. The kick was wide, and Pitt fans were stunned into silence.

Then they got another chance. Cavanaugh threw a long pass to the Lion 35. It was incomplete, but the Lions were called for interference. Cavanaugh then passed to Karl Farmer on the 25. With nine seconds left, Farmer hopped out of bounds to stop the clock.

Out came Carson Long again. This was it! "He can't miss three in a row!" Even the Penn State fans were saying that. The Panthers were finally going to beat Penn State!

Long kicked . . . short! He couldn't believe it. Nobody could. The game was over, and Penn State had jinxed the Panthers again.

Poor Carson Long was asked how he felt. "Horrible," he said.

Tony came to his defense. "I know how Carson feels," he said. "Remember, I fumbled on the 1-yard line at Notre Dame last year and we lost the game."

Tony had his best yardage yet against Penn State, with 125 yards on 28 carries. He ended the season with an amazing 1,544 yards rushing, which made him 4,234 yards in three years. That didn't make him feel any better about losing to Penn State again, though. Sometimes in football you could do everything right, he sighed, and still come out on the wrong end of the score.

Well, there was the Sun Bowl to look forward to on December 26th. Spending Christmas in the sunny weather was fun, and the game turned out to be fun, too. Haygood was back at quarterback and he rushed for 101 yards. Walker had 123, and Tony ran for 142. Nobody could remember the last time three Pitt backs had rushed for more than a hundred yards in a game. The Panthers won easily, 33–19. Tony was back as a first team All-American, and was named UPI Eastern Player of the Year.

TONY DORSETT

Now, wait till next year!

Something Johnny Majors had told Ed and Tony back in Coach Ross's dining room didn't seem so funny now. That was a chance at the national championship.

Now, that seemed possible. In fact, the Panthers were planning on it.

Of course, a lot of things could go wrong before a team won the national championship. . . .

CHAPTER XIV

The 1976 football season started at Pitt as soon as the Sun Bowl was over. The Panthers were going for the national championship, and the pressure built up fast.

For the team, the excitement was like a little kid waiting for Santa Claus to come. But it was heavier than that, too. It was more like the Pitt football team was running for President of the United States.

The pressure was even heavier on Tony, because he really was a candidate, for the Heisman Trophy. To win that trophy as the best football player in the country meant winning the votes of sportswriters from the South and West as well as the North and East. Many of the writers would have their own regional favorites, and Tony would have to have another outstanding year to convince them he was the best.

Tony had been 11th in the Heisman voting his freshman year when he had rushed for more yards than the winner, Penn State's John Cappelletti. He was 13th in his sophomore year, and last year he was fourth, and outrushed the winner, Ohio State's Archie Griffin. This year was going to be the year of the Hawk!

For Tony's senior year, Sports Information Director Dean

Billick was getting 10 to 20 requests for interviews with Tony every week, and Tony never turned them down. "I guess I'd be upset if nobody wanted to talk to me," he said.

His schedule became so hectic that Billick had to set up certain days for him to meet with reporters. Tony spent every Tuesday and Thursday afternoon meeting with them, usually with several writers at once. He enjoyed that, in a way. It was a challenge.

Billick made sure that Tony's name was never mentioned without the words, "Heisman Trophy Candidate" beside it. He didn't want to publicize just Tony's running statistics— those spoke for themselves. "We want to show his personality, too," he said, "because he's a great person."

Tony was used to being in a crowd on the football field; he couldn't go for a drink of water without two tackles and a linebacker following him. Off the field, he could scarcely eat breakfast without a reporter.

At the same time, he couldn't be with his buddies as much as he wanted to. The Panthers were a close-knit bunch, and they liked to go out together to some favorite hangouts. But Tony finally had to stop going with them. Something about him—his fame, his good looks, his big eyes and quick grin—drew people to him. Before long, he'd be surrounded by such a crowd it ruined the good time for the rest of the team.

After practice, there was always a crowd of reporters waiting to talk to him. The other Panthers wondered how he stood it. But Tony knew that this was his bread and butter now, his future. He often stayed for two hours after practice or a game to talk to the writers, while Dean Billick waited to drive him home.

"I never once saw him try to duck anybody," said Bill Hillgrove. "I never saw him try to get out of there and say, 'Hey, my time's valuable.' He wouldn't even take a shower till all the reporters had left."

TONY DORSETT

After three years, though, all the ordinary sports-type stories had been written about Tony. Many magazines, newspapers, and all three TV networks wanted to do in-depth studies on him. They wanted to follow him around for a week. When Tony went to class, it was like a parade.

He took it all cheerfully. "You have to pay for your education somehow," he shrugged. He paid with his privacy.

Sometimes when people pressed him too much he'd fight back a little, just with his sense of humor. Tony was always good at putting people on while still looking perfectly serious. Once he told a reporter that he should be taller than he was now. "I used to be 6 feet tall," he said, "but I've been pounded down an inch on the football field." Some people believed him.

It was hard to be "on" all the time, and Tony needed a place he could be alone sometimes, so he took an apartment off campus for his senior year. He loved to listen to rock music on his stereo and just relax by himself. Much as the other Panthers liked him, none of them wanted to room with him. They'd seen what happened in the dorm—the phone ringing all day long and half the night, photographers in the hall, autograph hounds lying in wait, reporters hanging around the room. Nobody else wanted that hassle.

When he tried to take some time just for himself, there were always people who started saying he was unfriendly. Or, they said, maybe success had gone to his head.

"No, he's still the same Tony Dorsett," said one of his teammates, "and I don't know how he keeps his head together as well as he does."

"It's a wonder he even knows who Tony Dorsett *is*," agreed a Pitt coach, "but he hasn't changed."

Dean Billick was proud of the way Tony handled all this attention, and he was proud of the way he had matured in his years at Pitt. "I've seen him grow up right before my eyes," he said.

TONY DORSETT

From a 155-pound, lanky freshman, Tony was now listed at a solid 192 pounds. And, man, he was anxious to get the season started. He wanted to play football!"

So did the rest of the Panthers. The long buildup for the 1976 season should have made them tight, self-conscious, extremely nervous. Not the Panthers. They were loose and good-humored. They practiced hard and long but, well, they knew they were good. They had confidence in themselves. Better still, they had confidence in each other.

"We're practicing every day against the best defense in the country," said an offensive lineman. "That makes *us* better all the time."

With eighteen of twenty-two starters back from last year, football analysts couldn't find a weakness at any position. "Pitt is loaded with talent," said the *Pittsburgh Courier*, "and will be able to replace just about anyone in the lineup with a quality player, with the exception of Tony Dorsett."

The first game was coming up fast, even faster than expected. Notre Dame was moved up from the middle of the schedule to be played as the first televised game of the season, on September 11th. Going out to South Bend wouldn't be the easiest way to start a run at the national championship. Notre Dame was ranked 13th in the country in preseason, while Pitt was now ranked 9th. Losing this game could push the Panthers so far down in the ratings they'd never get up to Number One.

Tony showed he wasn't as tense as people expected him to be by showing up for the trip wearing a Kelly green suit—Notre Dame's color—just for fun. And Coach Majors showed that he knew what he was doing when he named his co-captains for the game.

In the visitors' locker room before game time, Majors announced their names—Ed Wilamowski and Tony Dorsett! Ed and Tony just looked at each other while a slow smile spread across their faces. It was something like the smile of a hungry man just before he tears into a big, thick juicy steak.

Coach Butch Ross was in the stands that day. When he saw Tony and Ed walk out on the field for the coin toss he thought he would never have a prouder moment. Those two boys he had coached in high school, co-captains of a team going for the national championship . . . for a high school coach, it was a real dream come true.

But when the game started, it looked like it might turn into another nightmare, like the game at Sharon. On their first possession, the Irish marched 86 yards. And scored!

Groans made the air turn blue around TV sets all over western Pennsylvania. Notre Dame students marched around carrying a big banner that read, "Hail Mary full of grace, Tony Dorsett's going no place!"

Oh, yeah? On Pitt's first play from scrimmage, Tony followed his blockers out through the line. He swooshed past the linebackers and bobbed and weaved through the secondary. Nobody caught him till he was forced out of bounds at the Notre Dame 23-yard line—61 yards from where he'd started!

A clipping penalty put the ball back to the 31. Robert Haygood picked up 6 yards, then passed to Jim Corbett at the 5. From there, Tony whizzed around the right end, and scored!

The Pitt defense now began to amaze people who hadn't noticed they were around before. They intercepted four Irish passes and knocked down more.

Tony kept on running, and running, to the tune of 181 yards, and Pitt stomped the Irish 31–10.

Named as offensive player of the game was Tony Dorsett, ex-Hopewell Viking. Defensive player honors went to tackle Randy Holloway, ex-Sharon Bengal. The MAC looked all right in the big time!

After the celebration had calmed down, about three days

later, Coach Majors had to inject some realism into his players. "It's something to build on, not to sit on," he said about the big victory. "We'd better get some work done this week. We've got a lot to improve on."

Down in Atlanta, Georgia, Coach Pepper Rodgers was hoping the Panthers wouldn't do any improving. His Georgia Tech team had just lost to South Carolina and he wasn't looking forward to playing a team that beat Notre Dame and then got better!

Robert Haygood's hometown of East Point, Georgia, was not far from Atlanta, and he was looking forward to a great homecoming in front of his hometown friends. But it was Pitt's big defensive line that showed off first in front of the 43,000 screaming Georgia Tech fans. Tackles Randy Holloway and Don Parrish, nose guard Al Romano, and ends Cecil Johnson and Ed Wilamowski kept pushing the Tech Yellow Jackets farther and farther back. Larry Swider kept them there with punts of 60 and 77 yards.

Parrish sacked the quarterback and recovered a Tech fumble in the first quarter. Haygood was making his dream come true when he ran for 36 yards to the Tech 10. Tony slashed over from there, and Pitt was leading 7–0.

But, in the second quarter, tragedy struck Haygood. Trying to make a cut, he slipped and fell. He had to be helped off the field.

The Panther front wall came back at the Yellow Jackets and knocked the ball out of runner Eddie Lee Ivory's hands. Ed Wilamowski recovered. A few plays later, Tony ran around the right end for another touchdown.

In the second half, as the newspaper had once said about the game against New Castle, it started raining Hopewell Vikings . . . and now it rained Pitt Panthers. The final score was Pitt 42, Georgia Tech 14. Tony had 113 yards and three touchdowns.

But the news from the doctors was bad. Haygood had

Ed Wilamowski takes to the air on defense for Pitt. (*Photo courtesy Sports Information Office, University of Pittsburgh*)

torn the cartilage in his knee. He was out for the season; it was probably the end of his career.

That loss saddened the whole team. And now Matt Cavanaugh had to take over the quarterback job. He had come through as a passer against Tech, with seven completions out of thirteen tries. Still, it was just as well the first home game, with Temple, was going to be a breather. . . .

But the Temple Owls didn't seem to know they were a breather. In the first quarter, they put such a rush on Larry Swider that his punt was blocked. A Temple player grabbed the ball and ran 15 yards into the end zone, to give Temple the lead at 7–0. The player's name was Chuck Gill. At Temple, the Philadelphians said Gill was from some steel mill town out West. It was called Aliquippa, or something.

Gill remembered playing midget football with a skinny little kid they used to call "Hawkeye." The Hawk wasn't all that glad to see him again right now!

Then Temple fumbled, and Bob Jury recovered for Pitt on the Owls' 18. Tony ran for 11 yards, and went into the line on the next play. But he got up slowly, and then limped off the field. He had a big, painful bruise on his calf.

Pitt fumbled on the next play and didn't score. Later, Carson Long kicked a 50-yard field goal. And when the Panther defense forced a fumble on the Owl 38, Ed Wilamowski recovered. Tony threw the ice off his leg, went in and gained 20 yards, then limped back off the field. Long kicked another field goal.

At the half, Temple was leading 7–6. One of Pitt's problems was that Temple coach Wayne Hardin had come up with some trick plays, especially on punts. The Owls would look like they were going to run the ball on fourth down, then they would rush in the punter at the last second. The Panthers were getting so mixed up trying to get their kicking teams either in or out that once they drew a penalty for having sixteen men on the field!

TONY DORSETT

In the locker room, Majors gave the team a talking-to which was only described as "refreshing." The offense came out and put on two long scoring drives to finally win the game 21–7.

Between ice packs, Tony ran for 112 yards to make ten 100-yard games in a row. Now he needed only 80 yards a game for the rest of the season to break Archie Griffin's all-time college rushing record. But Tony wouldn't be satisfied with just breaking it. He wanted to go way over the mark, so there wouldn't be any doubt about who was the best runner ever!

Opposing defenses weren't buying that one, though. They were stacking linebackers in front of him and putting up eight- or nine-man lines so he couldn't get around them. Tony was taking a terrific pounding every week. Luckily, his leg injury wasn't serious. It would pain him for the next couple of weeks, but it wouldn't keep him down. One coach explained why Tony's injuries usually weren't the serious kind. "He's like Muhammad Ali—he's always moving away from the punch!"

Pitt had moved up in the polls now. They were second only to Michigan. Every team they played would be "up" for them, and every team wanted to stop Dorsett.

For the Duke game the next Saturday, the Pitt coaches decided to fool the defense by adding a new wrinkle to the quarterback's options. Instead of sliding down the line to the end, Cavanaugh would go only halfway. He'd stop suddenly, and dump a pass over the line.

At Duke, the grass was slippery after a morning rain. When Duke came in with a nine-man line, Pitt's running game was floundering. Into the second quarter, Tony hadn't even gained 5 yards. The Duke crowd started chanting, "Who is Tony Dorsett? Who is Tony Dorsett?"

Suddenly, Cavanaugh slid halfway down the line, stopped, and passed over the middle to his tight end, Jim Corbett.

Duke was surprised. Duke was astonished. Duke was helpless. By halftime, Pitt had scored 30 points to Duke's 7.

The Duke defense had to drop back and open up the line a little, and Tony was able to get some room to run. He ended the game with 134 yards and one TD. Cavanaugh set a new Pitt record with five touchdown passes, and Pitt won 44–31.

Reporters crowded around Tony in the locker room as usual. But when tackle George Messich brought his eight-year-old cousin in to meet Tony Dorsett, Tony asked the reporters to wait, while he talked to the boy first.

The happy Panthers headed home to play Louisville next week. That game was slated to be another breather. It turned out to be the kind of breather that could wreck a national championship.

CHAPTER XV

The Louisville game started out as a real breather. The Panthers were leading 27–0 at the half. Tony had already rushed for 109 yards and Cavanaugh for 63.

But then Cavanaugh went down. It looked like he might have a broken bone in his foot, and X-rays later showed that's what it was.

Now the Panthers were in real trouble. They had everything—brilliant defense, a great offensive line, the outstanding runner in the country. But they didn't have a quarterback.

And Majors had to send in a quarterback. Right now. He looked around and finally called on Tom Yewcic. Tom who?

In the Pitt press guide, Tom didn't even have a jersey number. He wasn't exactly the third-string quarterback, he was more like ninth-string. He was a walk-on, without a scholarship. He had been quarterbacking the scout teams—the squads that ran opponents' plays against the Panthers in practice—and he'd never taken a snap from regular center John Pelusi. Pelusi was out with an injury today, too, so now there were new players at both center and quarterback.

With a wet field, and a lot of jangling nerves, the Panthers went on. Yewcic had what Dean Billick called a "rough initiation." But the Panther defense held Louisville to 6 points. The offense struggled through, and Pitt won 27–6.

Tony had rushed for 130 yards, but now more was going to be asked of him. Cavanaugh would be out for at least three weeks. Nobody said so, but everybody knew it—Pitt's success was now up to Tony Dorsett!

With a new quarterback who hadn't practiced the Veer, the offense would have to be simplified. All week, the offense worked on the good old I-formation. They lined up with Hutton or Walker behind Yewcic, and Tony in his old place as the dot on the "I." Most of the plays would be hand-offs or pitchouts to Tony.

Tony didn't mind that. "The I is a good formation," he said. "I can explode with it."

And, facing a strong team from Miami University, he knew he'd have to. Yewcic was as ready as anybody could be after one week of practice, and the rest of the Panthers were high with determination to help him and give him confidence.

Seeing both Haygood and Cavanaugh standing sadly along the sideline on crutches, the fans didn't know what to expect. But if noise could help Yewcic and push Tony forward, they were there to do it.

The Panthers started out carefully, almost too carefully. They were stopped twice near the goal line. But then Pitt defensive back LeRoy Felder broke through and tackled the Miami quarterback behind his goal line for a safety. Pitt led by two points. Soon Tony slammed over from the three, and Pitt led by nine.

Toward the end of the second quarter, Tony did explode —44 yards! Three plays later, he took a screen pass from Yewcic. He ran left, then reversed. He cut back to the right sideline, cut around, accelerated, slowed to fake out a tackler, then put on even more speed. He went 40 yards, for his second touchdown.

TONY DORSETT

The run was "pure Dorsett," the papers said. Nobody else could have done it. Those full-speed cuts Tony could make seemed impossible to some people who watched him. To other people, they only seemed incredible.

The Panther defense kept knocking the ball loose and then falling on it. And they kept chasing the Miami quarterback and then falling on him, too.

In the fourth quarter, Pitt was leading 22–6. Larry Swider kicked his shortest punt of the year, only 26 yards. But Miami dropped it. George Messich recovered at the Miami 32. Tony ran for 22 yards, then Yewcic ran for 6. Now the Panthers showed they had been practicing something besides handoffs. Yewcic gave the ball to Tony, who handed off to flanker Willie Taylor in a reverse. Taylor went in for a touchdown.

Miami scored again on a long pass, but Tony wasn't through with them yet. On the first play after Miami's kickoff, he broke over the middle and never stopped. He ran 53 yards for another TD. The final score was 36–19, Pitt.

Johnny Majors was so relieved and excited he couldn't stop talking about how great everybody had been. "Considering the position we were in today, Tony Dorsett had the greatest day of any back I've ever seen," he said. "He took the pressure off a new quarterback. Our defense was magnificent, and this was a great day for Pitt football!"

Center John Pelusi added something else. "Love won today's game," he said, "love and togetherness. We knew what we had to do for the quarterback and Tom responded by doing a great job."

Tony had gained 227 yards against Miami, and now he needed only 158 yards to break the all-time record. Maybe he would do it next week, October 23rd, at Navy. After beating Pitt last year, Navy was about due for something, too—a dose of Dorsett's revenge.

Reporters streamed into Pittsburgh to talk to Tony about

his chances of breaking the record. Pitt fans fought and bargained for tickets to the game. Tony's family and many of his friends from home were coming. TV networks weren't covering the game, but one network decided to send camera crews to Annapolis, just in case Tony did it.

If the offensive line had love and determination last week, they doubled it for this game. All year, they had been setting goals for Tony. They wanted him to get at least 1,500 yards. If he was short, they yelled at each other to get with it, get him open this time. They wanted this record as much as Tony did.

The day was sunny in Annapolis, but the air was filled with electricity as though a thunderstorm were coming. The Navy defense was playing Tony tight, but there was no place to hide from Dorsett's lightning.

On Pitt's first drive, Tony gained 23 yards, but it took him eight carries to do it. The Panthers scored on a pass from Yewcic to Corbett.

Tony kept gaining. Ten yards, fifteen, six. . . . In the press box, Tony's total was announced after every play. In the second quarter, he scored from the six. He was getting closer . . . closer. . . .

The half ended with the score 14–0. The crowd was buzzing, and the locker room was filled with enthusiasm. "Let's get it now!" the Panthers yelled as they ran out of the locker room.

But when LeRoy Felder intercepted a pass on the Navy 29, the Panthers couldn't get a first down. Long.kicked a field goal. After the defense forced Navy to punt, Tony gained 5 yards to bring his total to 94. But it was Elliott Walker who broke through for the long one, and ran 69 yards for a touchdown.

On the next drive, Tony went over 100 yards with a 21-yard run through the middle. He broke a tackle and dived over the goal line. That took care of one record—he had just become the first player in NCAA history to gain a thousand yards in each of four seasons.

Coach Majors had more to think about than Tony's records, though. Well, there was the rest of the season. . . . He didn't want to risk Tony's getting injured. With a big lead in the fourth quarter, he wanted to take him out of the game.

But Tony was now up to 154 yards—four yards away from the record. "Do you want to break the record today?" Majors asked him.

"Yes," Tony said. "I'm here to play football!"

"All right," Majors decided. "I'll give you one more shot at it, then you come out."

The crowd was standing, screaming. Everybody on the Pitt side was jumping up and down. The Panther linemen were yelling at each other: "Let's get it for the Hawk!"

On the Navy 32, Tony took the ball from Yewcic. He raced around the left side. He broke one tackle, two, three. . . .

In the broadcast booth, Bill Hillgrove was saying, "Pitch back to the left, Dorsett hits the 30, the 25, the 15, the 10 . . . he's into the end zone for a Panther touchdown!"

"I was bananas by this time," Hillgrove remembered later. He announced, "Tony Dorsett has become the all-time leading rusher in the history of football, and even the Navy cannon has gone off!"

After that, he couldn't talk. He turned to his partner, Johnny Sauer, to carry him through, but Sauer had tears running down his cheeks, too. "We both lost it at that point," Hillgrove said.

Tony almost lost it, too. The whole Pitt team raced after him and jumped him in the end zone. Big Tom Brzoza knocked him down, and the rest of the Panthers fell on them and rolled over each other.

Tackles George Messich and John Hanhauser had planned

The record-breaking run against Navy, October 23, 1976. *(Photos courtesy Sports Information Office, University of Pittsburgh)*

His teammates carry Tony off the field and celebrate his breaking the all-time college rushing record. (*Photo courtesy Sports Information Office, University of Pittsburgh*)

to be the ones to carry Tony off the field, but that turned out to be a harder job than they thought. They had to lift half the rest of the team with him.

When Tony finally got out of the pile, he went over behind the Pitt bench and called his parents to come down on the field. He gave them both a big hug and kiss, and they all started to cry. "I'm the happiest guy in the world," Tony told his mother. "I'm the happiest person in the world," she said.

The TV network broke into its regular game to show Tony's run, and the Pitt-Navy game was almost forgotten. It was held up for 15 minutes. "Pitt has drawn a bench penalty of 15 yards for running out on the field," reported Bill Hillgrove, "but *it really doesn't matter!*"

Tony finally walked all the way around the field, behind the Navy bench, to wave to Hillgrove up in the booth. As he did, the entire brigade of Naval midshipmen stood and doffed their caps to Tony. "What a classy welcome," said Hillgrove. And, he said, "If I watch college football for another fifty years, I may never see one like Tony. He's a very special individual."

After the 45–0 victory, Coach Majors had Tony stand on a chair in the middle of the locker room. "Hawk," he said, "all this couldn't have happened to a greater young man and football player. You are the greatest football player I've ever seen!"

Tears streamed down Majors' face. And Tony's. And everybody else's. Looking at all the tears, Majors said, "I think that says a lot about how this team feels about Tony Dorsett."

Then Tony wanted to say something. "You guys are the greatest in the world. I love you for everything you've done to help me. You blocked for me, the defense got the ball to the offense, and we were able to do our thing!" The cheering just about brought down the walls.

TONY DORSETT

Majors and the Panthers had come a long way together. They had battled their way from the bottom to the top. Well, almost to the top. The season wasn't over yet. There was still somebody waiting every week to bring them down.

It was the Syracuse Orangemen who looked forward to bringing Pitt down next week at Pitt Stadium. They had only a mediocre 4–3 record, and Pitt fans didn't give them much of a chance at wrecking the Panthers. They did worry, though, about some other happenings, the kind of things coaches call "distractions."

Tony had more distractions than he needed, but he stayed cool through it all. He had magazine interviews, he appeared on TV, and he had to make speeches. He even rode an elephant to lead a circus parade!

Tuesday was just a typical day—almost. A visitor came to town and asked to meet Tony Dorsett. He wanted his picture taken with Tony. Well, anybody in Pittsburgh would have been glad to have a picture taken with Tony. He could spend all his time doing that if he wanted to. But this request was a little different. It came from Gerald R. Ford, President of the United States!

Now Tony, who had been too shy to talk to the college dudes four years ago, suddenly found himself in a car with Coach Majors, on his way to talk to President Ford. At the Greater Pittsburgh Airport, the President shook Tony's hand and congratulated him on breaking the record.

The President and Tony had something to joke with each other about. Mr. Ford had played center on Michigan's football team, and Michigan was still the only team ahead of Pitt in the national rankings. In his shy way, with the humor hidden underneath, Tony gave the President a blue and gold button to wear. The button said, "Pitt's No. 1!"

President Ford gave Tony a little surprise in return. He said he had been campaigning at the steel mill in Aliquippa and had just met Tony's father!

TONY DORSETT

On the way back from the airport, Tony had to stop at the weekly Pitt press luncheon, where he and Tom Yewcic were to make talks and answer questions.

Yewcic was asked what he had done on Tony's record-breaking run. "I just handed him the ball and settled back to watch him," he said. "It was a thrill just to hand the ball off to him."

When Tony told about his meeting with the President, one reporter said, "Within a year, you'll be making more money than the President!"

What? Well, all the experts thought Tony would be picked in the first round of the pro draft; maybe he'd even be the first player chosen. That would mean a fat contract.

A reporter asked Tony which pro team he'd like to play for. Tony didn't dodge the question. "I like Pittsburgh," he said, "and I've been a Steeler fan since I was a kid. But if it's not the Steelers, I'd like to play someplace where the weather is warm."

Even with all those things going on, practice still wasn't forgotten. What the Panthers didn't know was that Syracuse was going to spring a surprise.

CHAPTER XVI

The surprise Syracuse had for the Panthers was a sophomore quarterback named Bill Hurley who started passing and wouldn't stop. One of those passes was an 80-yard scoring bomb. At the end of the first quarter, Pitt was behind 7–3. The Pitt crowd of more than 50,000 started getting nervous.

Tony suddenly made them more nervous. He left the game. He took a hard hit, even though he didn't have the ball, and he heard his elbow pop. He was afraid it was broken.

But, when he found it wasn't broken, he had it wrapped like a mummy's and went back into the game. On a long drive he had gains of 33 and 15 yards. From the 2, he hit the line twice before he got over for a touchdown.

Syracuse threatened again before the half ended. They were down to the Pitt 6 before Ed Wilamowski recovered a fumble.

In the locker room, the coaches were nervous, but the players were still cool. "We had confidence in our defense," said an offensive lineman. "We knew they could hold them. And we knew Tony would break it open sooner or later."

After the half, Syracuse got two field goals in a row. The Panthers came back with a drive from their own 20. On the

Tony gives his jersey to President Gerald R. Ford while Coach
Johnny Majors watches. (*Photo courtesy Sports Information Office, University of Pittsburgh*)

TONY DORSETT

Syracuse 33, they took a chance. It was fourth and one. They decided to go for it.

Yewcic kept the ball and ran for four yards. He made the first down. Then he pitched out to Tony. With blockers knocking people out of the way in front of him, Tony raced all the way!

The Panthers thought this was the most physical game they'd played yet. The action on the line looked like the inside of a cement mixer. Tony had to leave the game more than once. He had a bruised leg, and then somebody poked him in the eye. There wasn't a place on him that didn't hurt. Still, he managed to carry the ball 34 times. At the end of the game, he went dodging and cutting downfield for runs of 28 and 33 yards. He set up a field goal with 27 seconds left. Pitt finally outlasted Syracuse to win 23–13.

When Tony's yards were added up, he had gained 241. That hardly seemed possible, with the injuries he'd had. Butch Ross wasn't surprised that he could do it, though, and neither were the Pitt coaches. They had seen him play, hurt, too many times before.

Next week was Homecoming at Pitt, with parades and pretty girls, and the Army. It was a good thing Army wasn't the strongest team on the schedule with half the Panthers limping and the other half with their arms in slings. The training room looked like a hospital. Even the players who weren't injured were sore all over. But somehow when Saturday came they all straightened up and ran out on the field as if nothing had happened.

The big Homecoming crowd saw what they had come to see this year—Tony running—for 212 yards. Quarterback Matt Cavanaugh came back, and passed for 67 yards. But before the Army surrendered 37–7, something else happened that set Pitt Stadium jiving.

Out in Indiana, Number One Michigan was playing at Purdue. Purdue, with a record of 3 wins, 5 losses, was giving

Michigan a shock. Michigan was behind 16–14. With fourteen seconds left in the game, Michigan tried a field goal, and . . . missed!

As soon as he had the word, Pitt's public address announcer came on the microphone. "In scores of other games . . . we have a final. . . ." He paused. "Michigan . . . 14. . . ." He paused again. You could have heard a hot dog wrapper dropping in Pitt Stadium. ". . . Purdue . . . *sixteen!*"

"Yeeeow! We're Number One!" The screaming could be heard almost to Aliquippa. Or, maybe, halfway to Morgantown, West Virginia. Over there, the sound of Pitt cheering was always the signal for another good old Hillbilly feud!

West Virginia had won only four games this year. They shouldn't have a chance against the undefeated Panthers. But whenever Pitt and West Virginia play, the record books go through the paper shredder.

As Tony passed the West Virginia bench at the start of the game, he flashed the "Number One" sign. He was daring them to do something about it. The Mountaineers strained like dogs on leashes to get at him.

Every time they caught him, they hit him—hard. But with the ball on the West Virginia 17, Tony did a zig and a zag off the right side and whizzed down the sideline for a touchdown.

When West Virginia recovered a fumble on the Pitt 22, Bill McKenzie, last year's hero, kicked a field goal. A 7–3 lead wasn't what the Panthers had in mind. The Mountaineers were stacking against Tony—bringing their linebackers in behind the tackle and the end and shutting off all Cavanaugh's options but one. That was the option with the quarterback keeping the ball and running with it himself. Cavanaugh was a slower runner—they'd rather have him running the ball than Tony.

TONY DORSETT

Cavanaugh ran better than they expected. He picked up some long gains. He didn't enjoy it, though. He said after the game, "Now I know how Tony feels, the way he takes a beating all the time. I have more respect for him than ever."

The Panthers scored, with Tony banging through the middle of the line from the 2. At the half, it was 14–3.

The halftime ceremonies featured something unusual today—a football player. A new jersey with the number 33 on it was presented to Tony Dorsett by Cas Myslinski, Pitt's Athletic Director, and University Chancellor Wesley Posvar. Tony's jersey was being retired. Nobody at Pitt would ever wear number 33 again. Butch Ross's wish had come true—he had lived to see it. Well, it hadn't taken nearly as long as he thought it would.

Later on, Pitt would retire Tony's locker, too. Equipment manager "Boo" Connors would keep Tony's equipment in it and in good shape, just as though Tony were coming back to play again. It would be an inspiration to many future Pitt players, and it showed how highly Tony was thought of at Pitt by everyone who worked with him.

Having his jersey retired was a big thrill for Tony, and for his family. But the Mountaineers weren't impressed. They came back gunning for him.

In the third quarter, the Panthers got to the West Virginia 10 on Cavanaugh's passing and running, then Long kicked a field goal. Then quarterback Dan Kendra short-passed the Mountaineers downfield for a touchdown.

Now Pitt led 17–10. Tony rubbed his bruises and got ready to go back in and get more of them.

After the kickoff, the Panthers were backed up to their own 13-yard line. But then Tony ran the ball four out of the next five plays, and the Panthers were out to the 39.

They were stopped at midfield, and Larry Swider came in

to punt. Then Pitt got a break. There was a clipping penalty on the punt against the Mountaineers. The Panthers got the ball on the Mountaineer 30.

Other teams were always jeering at Tony. They'd say, "Hey, Dorsett, you're no good!" And worse.

A teammate said, "Tony enjoyed getting back at them. We could see it in his eyes, building up. We loved it when he finally broke one."

Now was the time. Tony took the ball and swept right. He cut back. There were Mountaineers in front of him, beside him, and coming at him from behind. He ran past them, around them, and away from them. He put his moves on them and had them running the wrong direction. Two or three caught him, but he jerked away, and crossed the goal line all alone.

The Mountaineers weren't finished yet. They scored again late in the fourth quarter. On the kickoff, the Panthers were backed up again, this time to the 9-yard line. Tony carried the ball six times in a row. Five yards. Eleven yards. Eight yards. . . .

Finally, the Panthers were out to their 40-yard line with less than a minute left to play. The Mountaineers were trying desperately to get the ball. Right in front of the Pitt bench, Tony was stopped for no gain.

The play stopped, but the action didn't. A Mountaineer speared Tony in the back with his helmet, after the whistle had blown. Tony felt somebody pushing his fingers through his face mask, punching at his eyes.

For the first and only time in his whole career at Pitt, Tony lost his cool. He started swinging. He slammed the ball into a Mountaineer's helmet.

The Pitt bench ran out to help. There was a lot of pushing and shoving. Pitt coaches pulled Tony out of the mix-up, and the referees separated the pushers in a hurry. But they threw Tony out of the game!

TONY DORSETT

It was ironic—to get thrown out of his last game at Pitt Stadium. And it was even more ironic to find out that he had rushed for 199 yards. If he had been able to stay in for another play, he would have broken 200 yards again.

But, Tony said, "I am a man and a human being, and I can only take so much, then emotion takes over, especially in a game like this.

"I was getting a lot of dirty play laid on me throughout the ball game, and I was overlooking it. It was obvious to me he tried to spear me when I was down—he went for my head. I don't mind getting hit, but they were going for my eyes!"

The final score was Pitt 24, West Virginia 16. It was close, but the Panthers had come through again. The big game with Penn State wouldn't be played for two weeks, so they would have a chance to rest and get ready for the Lions.

But there were other distractions. A rumor started that Johnny Majors was planning to leave Pitt, that he might go home to coach at Tennessee.

Tony had a bigger distraction, too—the Heisman race. His closest competition for the trophy was Ricky Bell of Southern California, but Bell had been injured in mid-season and hadn't been able to keep up with Tony in the rushing race. Tony needed only 142 yards against Penn State to make his total 6,000 yards. That was something else no player had ever done.

And the bowl bids were coming in a week. To win the national championship the Panthers wanted to play the highest-ranked team they could. Michigan and Southern California were ranked Number 2 and Number 3, and they would be playing each other in the Rose Bowl. Georgia was ranked Number 4 and, as the Southeastern Conference champion, would be the host team in the Sugar Bowl in New Orleans. That was where the Panthers voted to go.

The Sugar Bowl bid was accepted with great pleasure by

Pitt officials. Pitt fans were running a fever in suspense and happiness.

Of course, the Panthers still had to beat Penn State.

"Watch Dorsett's feet," Joe Paterno was telling his Nittany Lions. "Don't watch his head or his shoulders or his hips—he'll fake you out!"

"That's right," said one Penn State defender. "His feet seem to go one way and his hips go another!" That made it hard for them to get solid hits on him the way they liked to. He was so slippery it was hard to punish him and wear him down, as the Penn State defense wore down other backs.

If the Panthers were having their greatest season, the Lions weren't. They had lost their first three games. But then they had come on to win all the rest and were heading for the Gator Bowl to play Notre Dame.

Most Panthers' memories went back over the past three years to all the losses to Penn State, and they planned to blow the Lions off the field this time. With Penn State, that was usually like trying to push a coal barge up the Monongahela River by blowing on it, but this year the Panthers were confident.

Besides, the Lions were way overdue for a lesson in Dorsett's revenge. But if any of the revenge's other victims —anyone from Sharon or Navy or West Virginia or Notre Dame—mentioned that to the Nittany Lions, they didn't pay enough attention.

The game was played on the Friday night after Thanksgiving, on national TV, at Three Rivers Stadium. Just up the Monongahela River from the stadium is a bridge called the Fort Pitt Bridge. Every afternoon at five o'clock, nine lanes of rush hour traffic suddenly merge into four lanes on that bridge. Violence and mayhem often result.

As Tony tried to carry the ball in the opening plays against Penn State, it looked as if he were caught in the middle lane of that bridge, with the other eight lanes of traffic bearing down on him. Violence and mayhem resulted.

In his first five carries, Tony gained only 6 yards. Then Penn State scored on a pass. On the kickoff, the Panthers took the ball at their own 2-yard-line. Tony gained 5 yards in 2 tries. Cavanaugh lifted a long pass to Gordon Jones, but then the traffic caught up with the Panthers again, and they had to punt.

Finally, Cavanaugh's passing cleared some of the traffic away from the line. Tony had a little more room. From the Lions' 13, it took Tony three plays to score. At the half, it was 7-7.

The Pitt fans were mumbling to themselves. Was Penn State going to jinx them again?

CHAPTER XVII

In the locker room, the Panther coaches were "making adjustments." They were trying to outwit Penn State by moving their men around on the gridiron, as a chess player does when he moves the chess pieces to different positions on the board.

"You always try to outnumber the defense at the point of attack," explained a coach. "When they stacked against Tony—put extra men in front of him—we tried to counter with extra men at that point, too. Or, we attacked at another point where we could outnumber them. If we could get Tony one-on-one with any defender, we knew he could beat him."

In the first half, the Pitt coaches had noticed that holes were opening up in the Lion defensive line for the fullback, but just for an instant. In that instant, a runner like Tony Dorsett could explode through. The coaches decided to try something new.

On some plays, Tony would line up at fullback, right behind Cavanaugh and closer to the line. To give him more protection, and to fool the defense, they also changed their offensive line from a balanced set to an unbalanced one, with both tackles lining up on the same side of the center. It was a formation they had used only a few times all season.

TONY DORSETT

The new offensive line set surprised the Lions. While they were trying to adjust to it, here came number 33 suddenly lining up in the fullback slot. Some observers thought the new formation confused the young Penn State players. "No," one of them said. "At fullback, Dorsett was just quicker than anybody else. And we were really messing up!"

Whatever it was, Tony was starting to motor. He zoomed through the middle in the third quarter for a 40-yard TD. Elliott Walker had a touchdown, and Long kicked a field goal. He hadn't forgotten last year, and probably never would. When the kick was good, he did a frog jump into the air and turned over in a somersault. Majors gave him the game ball after Pitt won 24–7.

Tony ended the game with 224 yards. That gave him 1,948 for the year and 6,082 for four years. "It's gonna take some effort to break those records," he admitted happily.

"Tony is the greatest athlete I've ever seen," said Ed Wilamowski. "If he doesn't win the Heisman Trophy, then there's no justice. Having only lived a couple miles away from him most of my life, I know how intense he is about football. There's probably not a harder worker around."

Johnny Majors said almost the same thing as reporters crowded around him in the locker room. "He's the greatest practice player I've ever had," he said. "He's all seriousness out there. That's what makes him such a great football player."

And, Majors added, "Beating Penn State was the biggest thrill of my life to date, but Tony Dorsett has given me more than enough thrills to last me a long time."

Even Majors, who had been talking nonstop since he came to Pitt, finally ran out of things to say. "There just aren't words to express how I feel about Tony Dorsett," he said.

Now it was on to the Sugar Bowl and that mean Georgia Junkyard Dog defense. But, for Tony, this week was a big one. The Heisman winner would be announced on Tuesday. Dean Billick thought Tony should have won it in his freshman and junior years, too. "He took this football team and carried in on his broad shoulders for four years," Billick said.

Pitt fans agreed. "Not since Red Grange has one player meant so much to a football team," said one.

But Tony was still nervous. The Heisman voters from the West might have gone for Ricky Bell—or something else could still go wrong. It wasn't easy to sleep the nights before the announcement.

When the call came, it was everything Tony had hoped for. He won the Heisman, 2,357 points to 1,346 for Ricky Bell. Tony won in every section of the country.

On Monday night, Majors, Tony and others from Pitt were in New York City to accept the Lambert Trophy as the best football team in the East. They appeared on the Today Show and went to the Downtown Athletic Club for the official Heisman announcement.

As Tony walked into the Heisman Room there, he was hit by a wall of bright lights and noise. TV lights shone in his eyes. Flashbulbs popped. Reporters fired questions at him as fast as machine gun bullets. It was a good thing he'd had four years of preparation for such a thing.

Tony answered questions as carefully and honestly as he always did. He said his most important goal was to see Pitt named the top team in the country. He said he had worked for the Heisman Trophy for a long time, but, "It goes home with me and only I can look at it. The national championship is something all of us can share."

He said he couldn't wait to bring his parents and his family back to New York for the Heisman banquet on December 9th. He wanted them to share in this award, and, he said, "We're going to be one big, happy family on December 9th!"

Tony with his parents Myrtle and Westley Dorsett after a game. (*Photo courtesy Sports Information Office, University of Pittsburgh*)

Myrtle Dorsett called Butch Ross and told him, "You and Mrs. Ross are going to the Heisman banquet with us!" Ross and Tony had stayed close friends over the years. Ross always sent him a telegram when he had a good game or broke a record, and Tony appreciated that. "You never forgot me," Tony said to him once.

Before the big group from Pitt and Hopewell took off for New York again, Coach Majors made an announcement. He had decided to take the coaching job in Tennessee and would leave Pitt after the Sugar Bowl.

Jackie Sherrill was named to replace Majors as head coach at Pitt. Sherrill had left the year before to be head coach at Washington State, but the players were glad to hear he was coming back.

TONY DORSETT

"Do you think you can recruit as well as Johnny Majors did?" reporters asked Sherrill.

"I recruited Tony Dorsett," Sherrill answered. No more questions like that were asked.

Those announcements didn't ruin the team's preparations for the Sugar Bowl, and they didn't spoil Tony's good time in New York, either. First there was a private luncheon to honor Tony and past Heisman Trophy winners. Tony cut a big cake which had a football and a stadium made of icing. On the cake were the words, "Hawk, Heisman, 1976."

That night, more than a thousand guests attended the banquet in the Hilton Hotel ballroom. The main speaker was none other than Penn State coach Joe Paterno. Looking at Tony, Paterno said that great opponents deserve your love, for forcing you to extend yourself and play your very best.

Paterno also kidded Johnny Majors about leaving Pitt. "If I had my choice, John," he said, "I'd rather have Dorsett leaving. He is the greatest football player we have ever played against at Penn State. In my twenty-seven years there, we have played against some awfully good ones—Jimmy Brown, Archie Griffin, Bubba Smith, and Greg Pruitt. But Tony Dorsett is the outstanding football player in America, and it isn't even close!"

Ronald G. Cobleigh, president of the Downtown Athletic Club, presented the big bronze trophy to Tony, and the crowd gave him a standing ovation. Tony introduced his family—his mother and father, his brothers, Ernest, Tyrone, and Keith, and their wives, his sister Juanita and her husband the Rev. Richard Kimbrough, and his youngest sister Sheree. He thanked everybody who had helped him along the way, and the Heisman electors for voting for him.

"This award is very symbolic to me," he said. "It means a lot to youngsters throughout the country who look up to the Heisman Trophy winners as I did when I was a child.

TONY DORSETT

I hope the good Lord will help me live up to such an outstanding award."

It was an evening none of the Dorsetts would ever forget. But Tony hardly had time to enjoy it. He always seemed to be the center of a crowd, of reporters, of people wanting his autograph, and even of strangers who wanted to use his name in business deals. Tony knew he had to be careful of those people.

As the Heisman representative, there were many speaking engagements Tony had to take on, too. He was jetting around the country so much that people wondered if he'd be in shape to play football on New Year's Day.

Tony smiled till his face felt like it would crack and talked till he didn't care if he never had to say another word. He was worn out. And now it was time to go to the Sugar Bowl.

The Panthers were leaving for their training center in Biloxi, Mississippi, on December 21st. For the first time since he'd been at Pitt, Tony asked Dean Billick not to schedule any interviews for him. He said he was exhausted and needed the time to practice.

"Okay, Hawk," Billick smiled. "You go play football. We'll do the interviews in New Orleans."

In Biloxi it was great just to settle down and practice with the team again. Every day, Tony stayed after practice to run for an hour. He didn't run alone. About a hundred local youngsters collected around him and ran along with him. What a thrill it was for them to run with the Heisman winner!

Tony enjoyed it, too. Laughing and kidding with the young boys, Tony signed autographs without losing a step.

Many of the Pitt coaches stayed to watch him. They were so proud of him they could hardly talk about it. Bob Matey couldn't help laughing when he remembered how the defensive coaches had wanted to put Tony on the defensive

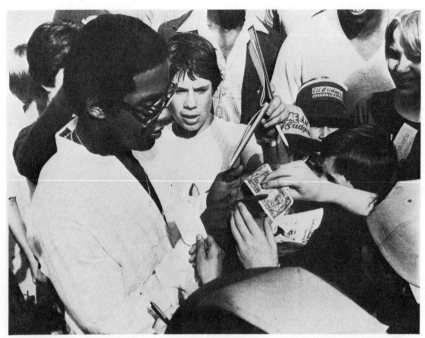

TD signs autographs for his best buddies and greatest fans—the kids. (*Photo courtesy Sports Information Office, University of Pittsburgh*)

team when he came to Pitt. "Can you imagine that mistake?" he smiled. "I'd be back home selling hot dogs right now!"

"But," he added, "Tony would have been the greatest defensive back in the country, too!"

There was more than practice for the team, too. They went on a deep-sea fishing trip, and they had a shrimp broil. On Christmas afternoon there was a big dinner and party.

The next morning, the Panthers boarded a bus for the city—the old and, to northerners, strange city of New Orleans. After checking into their hotel, the Panthers were treated to a riverboat ride on the Mississippi. They thought it wasn't so different from a ride on the Monongahela, except for the big ships flying Russian or Greek flags. Seeing

TONY DORSETT

Russian letters on the side of a ship made the river seem foreign and exotic to people who were used to seeing "U.S. Steel," or "Jones & Laughlin" on riverboats pushing coal barges.

After practice, the Panthers had plenty of time to tour the city. They often shocked the proper southern sportswriters who gave up trying to follow them as they took in the night life of the city's ancient French Quarter. Along its world-famous Bourbon Street, the sound of Dixieland jazz filled the air, and Georgia fans yelling, "Dog Meat!" filled the street.

The Panthers' hotel was also the headquarters for the Georgia fans, so the Pitt team had to listen to "Dog Meat!" wherever they went. One night Tony and Coach Bob Matey were cornered in an elevator by a group of Georgia fans. They recognized Tony. "We're gonna make dog meat out of you, Dorsett!" they yelled in his face.

Tony and Coach Matey just looked at each other in disgust. But as Tony left the elevator he turned and said, "You better be glad *you* won't be out on that field against us!"

Tony did appear at press conferences and answered the same old questions patiently. And he surprised one Georgia reporter by giving him a short lesson in the Dorsett philosophy. The reporter asked him how he had been able to carry the ball twenty or thirty times a game without being injured seriously.

"Three things," Tony said. "Excellent teammates, good coaching, and the good Lord!" There was a lot of Myrtle Dorsett's teaching in that answer.

While the Dorsett family was enjoying New Orleans with other Pitt fans, they could all feel the tension building up. The fans were happy and confident, but sometimes the tension would catch them. They'd blame the feeling on eating too much shrimp or too many grits.

On the night before the game, Majors called for a ten

o'clock curfew. "We would have come in that night, anyway," said one Panther. "We were ready to play!"

That night, the Georgia fans held a giant pep rally—at the Panthers' hotel! Some of the Panthers walked through the lobby and laughed when people stopped them to talk about grinding them into dog meat. Some players couldn't even get through and had to sneak into the hotel through the basement and go up the freight elevators.

The next day, the Panthers were up and out early. The game was to start at 11:30 A.M., New Orleans time. From the bus that took them the short drive to the Superdome, they could see red shirts and red and black pom-poms everywhere.

"Dog Meat!" followed them down the street. The team had never been so anxious for a game to start.

CHAPTER XVIII

There was something unreal about playing in the Superdome. Maybe it was being under a roof. Maybe it was the huge TV monitor hanging overhead. Maybe it was the mist fogging the air, drifting down from the dome. Maybe it was just the collected nervousness of the more than 76,000 people bouncing in their seats.

Some fans thought the stadium looked like a football field in a dream. It seemed faraway and strange. It looked misty to Tony, too, as he went out on the field for the coin toss. For him, it was because he had tears in his eyes. Oh, man—he did want to win this game!

But there were several things working against Pitt. New Orleans had been built on top of a swamp, and Eastern teams had been sinking in it since 1955, the last time an Eastern team had won the Sugar Bowl. Georgia had beaten powerhouse Alabama 21–0, and was rated almost even with Pitt for the game. Then there were those red-shirted fans. Had they intimidated the Panthers? The Superdome seemed to be filled with red, but the smaller number of Pitt fans tried to make up for that with noise.

What Tony had to do was shut everything else out of his mind. He had to shut out the Heisman excitement, the chance of losing the national championship right here on

165

this field, the nasty remarks thrown at him by the Bulldogs and their fans, the bass drums and the trumpets, the TV cameras. . . .

Tony just looked down the field and saw that goal line. That's what he kept his mind on.

Pitt won the toss, and Tony said they would receive. After the kickoff, he looked across his line and saw nine Junkyard Dogs pawing the turf and growling at him.

He ran at them for 4 yards up the middle on the first play. On the second, he lost 2 yards. Hutton gained 6, but Pitt had to punt.

The Pitt defense showed the Bulldogs something they'd already shown Notre Dame and Penn State—they were as tough and mean as Junkyard Dogs themselves. Maybe tougher. Georgia had to punt.

From the Pitt 20, Tony burst over left tackle for 5 yards. Then he ran around right end for 3. On the next play, he gained 2. First down.

Georgia was penalized 5 yards for being offside. Their fans howled at the referees. Walker then gained 6 yards for another first down.

On the Pitt 41, Cavanaugh pitched out to Tony. He lost 4 yards. He was hit hard and fumbled, but the play was already out of bounds. A pass to Gordon Jones gained 13 yards. Now the Panthers were on the 50-yard line. But it was fourth down, and one yard to go.

"Go for it!" the Pitt fans yelled.

The Panthers lined up. Fans on both sides were standing, screaming. There wasn't any kicker in there! The Panthers were going to gamble!

It looked like half the population of Georgia was standing in front of Tony Dorsett. The Bulldogs nabbed him quickly. But Cavanaugh still had the ball! He sneaked through the middle and gained 3 yards. First down!

TONY DORSETT

Now came the big one. Cavanaugh lifted a short pass to Walker. He ran up the middle for 36 yards. Cavanaugh then ran around left end for a touchdown! Panthers 7, Bulldogs 0. Early in the second quarter, Cavanaugh passed to Jones again. Jones broke a tackle and went all the way—59 yards for another TD!

Four minutes later, Pitt had the ball again. Walker carried three times for 13 yards. The Dogs shifted a little to take care of Walker. On the next play, Cavanaugh pitched out to Tony. He ran around left end for 22 yards.

Then, from the 11-yard line, Tony sped around right end for a touchdown. The half was almost over. Pitt was leading 21–0, and Georgia hadn't even completed a pass! The red-shirt section was getting very quiet.

Soon after the half, Georgia recovered a fumble on the Pitt 25-yard line. They kicked a field goal. But Tony soon showed the Bulldogs and their fans what he was famous for. He ran through right tackle and was gone before the Bulldogs knew he was missing. Pitt tackle George Messich blocked his man and felt Tony whoosh by. He looked up and saw Tony far downfield.

"His body was horizontal in the air, and he was still running!" Messich exclaimed.

At the Georgia 17, Jones threw a block on a defender, but the man rolled over him and knocked Tony out of bounds. But that 67-yard run showed the Junkyard Dogs who *wasn't* Dog Meat!

Long kicked a field goal and added another in the fourth quarter.

The final score of 27–3 made believers of all the doubters. Cavanaugh was voted the game's most valuable player. Tony, who rushed for a Sugar Bowl record of 202 yards, came in second, a point-and-a-half behind.

Pitt led in first downs, 24 to 14. They led in rushing, 288

yards to 135 for Georgia. In passing, Pitt had 192 yards to Georgia's embarrassing 46. In fact, Georgia completed only 3 passes of 22 tries in the whole game.

Georgia coach Vince Dooley said sadly, "I think Dorsett is faster than the last two times we played against him." Even Dooley had trouble believing such a thing was possible. But he had seen it.

Panther fans didn't have trouble believing anything now. A miracle had happened. They had watched it happen themselves, over the past four years.

After the game they went out hunting for those Dog fans who had been yelling in their faces all week. They just wanted to remind them of the final score, and who was the national championship team, and a few details like that. But they couldn't find any red shirts—they had all disappeared!

Anybody who saw Tony's face after the game knew what pure happiness looked like. All the players and coaches said the same thing—they just didn't know how to describe their feelings. To work so hard for four years, and win. . . . Well, it was just something they planned to tell their children and grandchildren about for the next fifty years!

The Panther locker room was a sweaty, steaming madhouse. Reporters crowded the Panthers till they could hardly find their lockers.

Tony finally appeared, dressed in a full-length raccoon coat! Two policemen met him, escorted him out of the stadium, and whisked him to the airport. He was on his way to play in the Hula Bowl in Honolulu, then on to another all-star game in Japan. It would be a fun trip.

But the two police bodyguards showed that Tony's life really was not his own anymore. They were a sign of things to come. His life after the Sugar Bowl was in the hands of agents and his fate as a pro player in the hands of many other people. He needed agents to handle the speaking trips and business offers that were pouring in. He needed them to negotiate a good contract with a pro team.

By the time Tony got back from Japan, his schedule was filled up with meetings, banquets, and speeches. School had already started, and it was too late to register for the last semester. Tony decided it was best to drop out of school for now.

Myrtle Dorsett didn't like that. Tony was so close to graduating, and she wanted him to get his degree. Tony promised that he would, some day. But right now, Tony Dorsett wasn't just a person any more—he was practically an industry!

CHAPTER XIX

Tony was waiting to be drafted by a pro team, but suddenly there wasn't any draft!

A law suit had put off the draft. There was a chance the draft wouldn't even be held. Then all the players would have to make their own deals with the teams they wanted to play for. For the top players, that might mean that teams would be bidding for them. A famous player like Tony could almost name his own price in that case.

While he was waiting, Tony wasn't sitting still. He was making public appearances all around the country, and now that the football season was over and he was turning pro, he was paid well for many of them.

One appearance was in Pittsburgh, at the Dapper Dan banquet, the most important sports banquet of the year, sponsored by the *Pittsburgh Post-Gazette*. Tony had been voted the winner of the Dapper Dan award, which goes every year to the sports figure who has done the most for the city.

Tony first introduced his parents. He said, "They are the most important people in my life." Then he talked about Pitt's championship season. "It started last summer when Pitt decided to change the schedule. A lot of people thought

170

it was a big mistake to change it and open with Notre Dame instead of Louisville.

"We beat Notre Dame impressively and went to Atlanta and beat Georgia Tech impressively and we lost our first-string quarterback. Then Matt Cavanaugh took the helm and we played three super games.

"Then Matt got hurt and a lot of people started to worry. I was worried, too. Then Johnny Majors, the good coach that he is, went into his bag of tricks and brought out the name of Tom Yewcic. There were a lot of doubts, and I had them, too, but Coach Majors has a saying that when your number is called, you should be ready. His number was called and he was ready.

"Some people counted us out before the Penn State game, and when we went to play Georgia in the Sugar Bowl. We were dog food, so to speak. And we won that game impressively."

Tony turned to Johnny Majors. "Coach Majors, a person exemplifies what he is by what he does, and your record speaks for itself. We enjoyed your short stay here, and I wish you all the success in the world.

"A few weeks ago I sat down to figure out the reason for the success I've had. It was the coaches and the athletes we had, but if anyone deserved the most credit, it was the Lord.

"Every night when I go to bed I thank the Lord, and I thank Him when I wake up in the morning."

Then Tony turned to Art Rooney, the owner of the Pittsburgh Steelers. "Mr. Rooney," he said, "I've had four wonderful years in the city of Pittsburgh. Please don't let me go!"

The crowd was first shocked by Tony's direct approach, then delighted by it. They stood and cheered for five minutes. Some Pitt fans in the crowd sobbed. They didn't want to let Tony go!

But if the draft was held, there was no way Tony could

play for the Steelers. The team with the worst record would pick first. The Steelers' record was too good—Tony would be long gone before they had a chance to draft him.

While Tony was nervously waiting, he went back to Hopewell for another big banquet. His hometown friends made him an honorary member of his dad's union local and declared him "the world's greatest running back!"

Nobody but Tony remembered when he was called "the sorriest Dorsett." Any time he drove into town, the people acted like a movie star had arrived. But if Tony saw an old friend on the street he'd stop and jump out of his car to have a good old hometown talk.

It was fun going around picking up awards and hearing everybody talk about how great he was. But now an agreement between the National Football League owners and players set the draft in motion again. It would be held in May.

Who would draft Tony?

The Tampa Bay Buccaneers had first choice in the draft. They were starting their second season and had not yet won a game. But Tampa Bay coach John McKay was planning to take one of his Southern California players first—Tony's rival, Ricky Bell. The second choice in the draft would go to the Seattle Seahawks. They were an expansion team like Tampa Bay and had a poor record of 2 wins, 12 losses.

Tony wanted to play for a better team than that, and his agent wrote to Seattle saying that Tony didn't want to come there.

Behind the scenes, there were plots and counterplots. It was like a big mystery movie, called, "Who Gets Tony?" And Tony just had to wait . . . and wait.

One of the plots was taking place in the offices of the Dallas Cowboys. The Cowboys had a great team, but they had not been able to win a Super Bowl yet. There was one thing they lacked—a breakaway runner. Hmmm . . . Tony

At the Hopewell banquet for "the world's greatest running back."
Ed Wilamowski; Marshall Goldberg, who set many running rec-
ords at Pitt; Coach Ross; and Tony. (*Photo courtesy Richard
"Butch" Ross*)

Dorsett was the greatest breakaway runner in the history
of college football. When Dallas put his records into their
computer, it almost blew a fuse.

Tony never knew it, but Dallas personnel director Gil
Brandt was watching him even in high school and always
liked what he saw. The Dallas men talked to the Seattle
Seahawks. Now the mystery movie had a subplot, called,
"Let's Make a Deal."

Seattle wanted Tony, but they needed more than one

runner to turn them into a good team. Dallas offered them several draft choices in return for their first-round pick. Seattle seemed to like the idea, but Tony was hearing only rumors. One rumor said he was going to the New York Jets, another said he was going to the Canadian League.

Finally, it was the day of the draft. Tampa Bay picked Ricky Bell. Then Seattle announced they had traded their first pick to Dallas for the Cowboys' first-round choice and three second-round picks. Dallas quickly chose Tony Dorsett. "I'm a Dallas Cowboy!" Tony yelled happily.

Nothing could happen to Tony any more without a press conference. He told the press, "It's a great situation to be in. The Cowboys are one of the contenders for the world championship. I have a chance to come right off a national championship at the collegiate level and go to a world championship at the pro level!"

Cowboy's President Tex Schramm said, "We were willing to sacrifice numbers—the draft choices—for one good football player. We think Tony is the most outstanding back that has come out of college since O. J. Simpson. We feel he could ignite a brilliant new era for the Cowboys."

Tony now had to wait some more while his agents negotiated the terms of his contract. Those talks had a happy ending. Although Tony's salary and bonuses were never announced, they were said to amount to more than a million dollars, to be spread over several years.

There was more than enough money to make Tony's childhood dream come true. He bought his parents that nice big house out in the country. The new house was not far from Aliquippa, since the Dorsetts didn't want to leave all their friends, and Tony wanted to come back there sometimes, too. He also bought himself some new wheels—a sleek, silver gray car with the license plate, "TD 33."

Now he had to make the team!

Johnny Majors predicted that would not be a problem.

TONY DORSETT

He said Tony would make the team the second day of practice. Well, the first day all they'd do was take pictures!

But just as some critics never thought Tony would make it in college, now they were saying he was too small for the pros. Could Tony run against, say, Mean Joe Greene? Forget it.

He reported with the other Dallas rookies to their training camp in warm and sunny Thousand Oaks, California. In spite of all his experience, he couldn't help acting a little like he had at his first camp at Pitt. He hung back, and some people again thought he was unfriendly. Tony had made so many headlines that people expected him to act big-headed. When he acted shy, they thought he was just being a snob.

And there was so much competition in a pro camp there was hardly time to be friendly. Tony, as the team's first-round draft choice, knew he didn't have to worry about being cut. But there were about sixty other rookies in camp —lower draft choices and free agents who had not been drafted—and they knew that only five or six of them would make the team.

Some of them tried to stay loose and joke about their chances, but others were grim. All of them feared that knock on the door, with a trainer saying, "Coach Landry wants to see you." That meant they were being cut.

That pressure made the camp much harder than college, but physically, it wasn't so different. On the first practice day, all the rookies had to run the "Tom Landry mile and a half." If they were too slow or couldn't finish, they might as well start packing their bags. Tony didn't have any trouble with that. He showed up well on the other exercises, too.

All the rookies were good football players or they wouldn't be trying out with the Dallas Cowboys. But when the veterans came into camp a week later, the rookies were scared.

TONY DORSETT

How could they compete with these legends—quarterback Roger Staubach; ends "Too Tall" Jones and Harvey Martin; tackle Jethro Pugh; wide receiver Preston Pearson; tight end Billy Joe DuPree, and running back Robert Newhouse!

These veterans were friendly, but they were tough. Tony Dorsett might be a legend himself, but they were going to make him prove he belonged here. They hit hard and didn't take it easy on the rookie who was supposed to lead them to the Super Bowl. Off the field, the meetings were just as hard. The Dallas offense was very complicated. Learning it was like going back to calculus class, Tony said.

Tony worked harder than he ever had, but somehow things weren't going as well as he hoped. He twisted a knee and that set him back almost two weeks. When camp was over, Tony hadn't made the first team!

"Tony is not having problems learning the system," Coach Tom Landry said. "He's just missed the repetition of running plays in camp."

When Tony's knee was back in shape, he played well in a few preseason games. But he was playing behind Preston Pearson, and not playing much at that.

Pearson, a dependable eleven-year veteran, was a good runner and pass receiver. He had played for the Pittsburgh Steelers before being traded to Dallas. He knew the system, and his years of experience put him far ahead of Tony. A runner with Dallas had to mesh with the other players, like cogs in a big machine. It took time to learn to do that.

Coach Landry didn't believe in pushing rookies too fast. He wanted to bring Tony along slowly, without skipping any of the steps of learning along the way.

With Pearson starting, the Cowboys beat the Pittsburgh Steelers 30–0 in an exhibition game in Dallas. The Pittsburgh newspapers said Dorsett was not a factor in the game. He gained only 34 yards in 12 carries.

Tony didn't complain. "I still have a lot to learn," he said.

Tony's face shows his game concentration as he runs around a tackle. (*Photo courtesy The Dallas Cowboys*)

TONY DORSETT

Against the Baltimore Colts, he had 99 yards. That was better!

But as the season started, Coach Landry announced his starters at running back—Robert Newhouse and Preston Pearson.

Maybe Tony wouldn't make it in the pros, after all!

CHAPTER XX

In his first game for the Hopewell Vikings, Tony gained over a hundred yards. In his first game for the Pitt Panthers, he gained 101. In his first regular season game with the Dallas Cowboys, he gained eleven.

Eleven yards?

Pitt Panther fans were shocked. TD could gain that many yards on one leg! What were they doing to him in Dallas? Why, they had only let him carry the ball four times!

The season opener was against the Minnesota Vikings, and it was a close one. Dallas won it 16–10, in overtime. The most valuable player was Preston Pearson, who had 63 yards in fifteen carries, and caught 5 passes.

Tony kept quiet. In a career filled with challenges, he hadn't failed to meet one, and he wasn't about to let this one get him down.

In the next game, the Cowboys ran over the New York Giants 41–21. Tony had only seven carries, but his total looked a lot better. He gained 62 yards. He also got his first Dallas touchdown on an 11-yard run. He was so excited he spiked the ball. Coach Landry didn't like that and let Tony know it. Tony would not do it again.

Tony wasn't comfortable as a part-time player. He hadn't been such a thing since the midget leagues! He dug in and waited. While Dallas was beating Tampa Bay 23–7, he played only on certain plays and downs, but he gained 72 yards.

The next week, he played a little more. And a little better. As Dallas beat St. Louis 23–7, Tony had 141 yards in only fourteen carries. That total was helped by breaking another record. From the Dallas 23-yard line, Tony started running. Suddenly, he was loose—all alone and showing these pros a sight Notre Dame had seen more of than they ever wanted—the number 33 disappearing into the distance. It was a 77-yard touchdown run, and it was the longest run from scrimmage in Dallas Cowboy history!

That was more like it, said the Dallas fans. Pitt fans relaxed, too. Tony was going to be all right!

Tony felt he had the complex Dallas plays down pat now. But he needed to carry the ball more. He usually got stronger the more he played—he needed to be in the game and get the feel of it, and then his natural running would take over.

But Coach Landry's schedule for Tony was slower than Johnny Majors' or Butch Ross's had been. He still wasn't ready to throw Tony in there for a whole game. With Pearson starting, the Cowboys were winning games. They beat the Washington Redskins 34–16, and Tony gained only 48 yards. After that, they downed the Philadelphia Eagles 16–10, with Tony gaining 48 yards again.

After the seventh game, a 37–0 whipping of the Detroit Lions, Tony had gained a total of 433 yards on eighty carries. In the next game, against the New York Giants, he gained only 29. The Cowboys won 24–10, with their great Doomsday defense sacking the Giant quarterback eight times.

Dallas had now won eight games in a row. Being on an undefeated team was great, but of course that was nothing

Tony is on his way for a Dallas touchdown. (*Photo courtesy The Dallas Cowboys*)

new to Tony. He hadn't been on the losing side in a game for two years now!

But, as Coach Ross had known, the only thing that really discouraged Tony was being taken out of a game. Now he was being taken out all the time. He had to fight his feelings of being discouraged and uncertain. He just worked harder.

The St. Louis Cardinals came into Texas in mid-November for another expected beating. But the Dallas offense had trouble getting started. Into the second quarter, they didn't have a first down. Then the Cowboy defense recovered a fumble on the St. Louis 21-yard line. And Tony came into the game. Roger Staubach passed to him. Ten yards; a first down. Then Tony ran for 4 yards. Next, it was 6 yards. Finally, he dived over the middle for a touchdown.

On the next Dallas drive, Tony carried six times for 20 yards, and Staubach passed for another TD. Dallas led 14–3 at the half.

But in the second half, the Cowboys' offense stalled again. The game got rough. Insults and punches were thrown on every play. Two players were put out of the game for fighting. And St. Louis came back with two touchdown passes late in the game to win 24–17.

The Dallas winning streak was broken. Their ground game had looked weak. Tony had gained 50 yards, but he had also caught three passes for 33 yards.

The Cowboys felt down after the wild game, and they had trouble getting up for the next one. The trouble was, another team was already up for it. That team was the Pittsburgh Steelers.

The Steelers had their famous "Steel Curtain," their front defensive four featuring Mean Joe Greene, who were noted for eating small running backs for breakfast. Like Tony Dorsett.

In Pittsburgh, the fans were looking forward to seeing Tony play again. They wanted to see him do well, but, ahem, well, darn it . . . they would root for the Dallas Cowboys about the time that palm trees sprouted along the icy Monongahela River.

Tony was happy to be going home to play at Three Rivers Stadium. He gave tickets to about a hundred of his friends and home folks. But he knew how Pittsburgh fans felt about the Steelers. Tony might be a favorite son in Pittsburgh, but when he showed up in a blue and white uniform, he'd be the enemy.

In the middle of the week, Coach Landry added to the drama by calling a press conference. Tony Dorsett would start the game, he said.

That was tough on Preston Pearson, who lived in Pittsburgh in the off-season. But Landry hoped Tony's starting before his old fans would give him and the team an extra spark.

Tony didn't know what to expect when he trotted out on the familiar turf at Three Rivers. He looked serious, a little worried. But then he looked up in the stands and saw a big banner which said, "Welcome Back Tony!"

As soon as the crowd spotted him, they jumped to their feet, almost from habit. They gave him a loud standing ovation. Tony smiled and waved back at them. And he showed them a little of his old stuff in the first quarter with a 14-yard touchdown run. He did that little dance in the end zone for his buddies, the way he'd done it once in high school.

"Hot dog!" yelled a Steeler.

"Yeah, I know it!" Tony laughed.

But there was nothing else to laugh about in that game. The Steelers' offensive line out-blocked the Dallas defense and sprung Steeler back Franco Harris for big plays and 113 yards. The Steel Curtain forced Dallas to pass and then knocked down the passes.

The Steelers won 28–13. The Pittsburgh sportswriters

were so spoiled by Tony's 200-yard games the year before that they wrote, "Dorsett didn't do much in this game." He only gained 73 yards!

After the game, reporters had a question for Coach Landry. "Will you start Tony Dorsett next week?"

"Yes," Landry said. "He's in there now."

Tony had finally made it. He had come through his initiation. Now he was a starter for the Dallas Cowboys! Of course, he had to keep the job.

At Washington the next week, Tony played a good game. He had 64 yards in nineteen carries, but none of his runs was for more than 9 yards. In the fourth quarter, he scored on a 1-yard run to give the Cowboys another win, 14–7. And Tony, along with Roger Staubach and other players, now needed a police escort just to get through the crowds to the team bus.

The next week the Philadelphia Eagles came to Dallas. The Cowboys rarely made headlines in Pittsburgh, but this time they did. The headlines said, "Dorsett Runs Wild!" Finally.

He scored first on a 1-yard run, then he took off for 84 yards. That broke his own record for the longest run in Dallas history. He gained a total of 206 yards and the 24–14 win clinched the Eastern Division National Football Conference championship for the Cowboys. They would play the Chicago Bears on December 26th in the first round of the playoffs.

But there were two games to play first. At San Francisco, the Cowboys had a passing contest with the 49ers on Monday night TV. Well, it was mostly passing. In the third quarter, a Dallas drive was mostly Dorsett. He caught a pass for 14 yards. Then he ran for 10. After that, he took a pitchout and ran for 21 yards and a TD. Howard Cosell exclaimed, "He doesn't run, he glides!"

Dallas finally won 42–35, and Tony had 92 yards. Now

"I'm a Dallas Cowboy!" (*Photo courtesy The Dallas Cowboys*)

he needed only 43 yards to have a 1,000-yard season. Maybe he would get that next Sunday against Denver.

But if the 49er game had been an offensive battle, the Denver game was the opposite. The Cowboys outlasted the Broncos to win 14–6. Tony had 50 yards, to make him 1,007 for the season.

He was named the NFC Rookie of the Year!

Tony had shown everybody he could make it in the pros. And, more important to him, he was now accepted by his teammates as an important part of the team.

Of course, he was looking ahead to something, the way he had looked ahead to the national championship last year. He was thinking about playing in the Super Bowl!

There were two playoff games first. In the first, the Dallas defense scrambled the Chicago Bears. Newhouse had 80 yards and Tony had 85. Tony caught a 32-yard pass and had a 22-yard touchdown run as Dallas won 37–7.

Next came the Minnesota Vikings, and the Dallas defense took over again. In the last quarter, Dallas was on the Minnesota 11. The Cowboys lined up in their shotgun formation, with the quarterback deep behind the center. Tony shifted position, as the Cowboy backs do on most plays. Although the shotgun is usually a passing formation, Tony cut across in a reverse. Staubach handed off to him, and he whizzed into the end zone for the Cowboys' last score. They won 23–6, to become the NFC champions. The Cowboys were in the Super Bowl!

If Tony felt he'd been here before, he had reason to. He was going to play in New Orleans as the NFC Rookie of the Year, for the pro football championship, and he would play on the same field he had played as the Heisman Trophy winner for the national college championship.

As Tony ran out into that misty Superdome, it was tempting to think back and remember the previous year. But he couldn't afford to do that. The Cowboys were playing the

The pros find Tony as hard to catch as the Sharon Bengals did.
(*Photo courtesy The Dallas Cowboys*)

TONY DORSETT

Denver Broncos, a team they had already beaten. But the Broncos had been underdogs all year, and they kept winning the big games. Instead of "Dog Meat," this year Tony was facing the "Orange Crush," and they were bigger and meaner than the Dogs.

The big Dallas defense started putting pressure on Bronco quarterback Craig Morton right from the start. The Denver offense started making mistakes. When Dallas intercepted a pass on the Denver 25-yard line, Staubach threw to Billy Joe DuPree on the 12. Then Newhouse ran for 2 and Tony went right for 6 yards. He gained another yard, and finally ran around the left side for 3 yards and a TD!

The Cowboys intercepted three more passes and recovered three fumbles, and led at the half 13–0.

In the second half, the Cowboys scored twice on passes. Even though Tony wasn't running as much as he would have been in college, Denver didn't like him being in the game at all. Just being there, he gave the Cowboys such a running threat that they had to guard against him. The cornerbacks had to come up closer to the line and that left the secondary more open for the passing game.

In the Sugar Bowl, Tony had gained 202 yards. In the Super Bowl, he gained 66 in fifteen carries. He was the rushing leader as Dallas won the Super Bowl 27–10.

For Tony, the victory was more than a dream come true. If a Hollywood script writer had written Tony's story into a movie, nobody would believe it could really happen.

As a skinny kid in a mill town, he had led the Hopewell Vikings to the MAC championship. Then he had taken Pitt's down-and-out football program and, as Dean Billick said, "carried it on his broad shoulders" to the national championship. To add winning the Super Bowl to all that was like something small boys think up in their daydreams. Tony had dreamed it too, once upon a time, and now it had all come true.

TONY DORSETT

But it hadn't just happened. Tony had made it happen. He had been born with a natural talent. From his mother he learned the pride and faith and determination that could make his dreams come true. On his strong legs, he not only ran away from the steel mill, he ran to the Super Bowl and a new life for him and his family.

In the future, Tony would have more football challenges, and would sign a movie contract. Whatever he tried, Tony would go on giving it the same extra effort he always did.

Any young football player who felt tired and discouraged, as Tony did many times, could watch him flash down the field and remember the extra effort behind that easy-looking stride. For Tony Dorsett, even when he was being called the greatest runner in the history of college football, always stayed after practice, to run.

And he always ran for the goal line.

ABOUT THE AUTHOR

Marcia McKenna Biddle is a Pennsylvanian herself and had an opportunity to talk at length with many of the people in Tony Dorsett's life. Mrs. Biddle writes a weekly newspaper column, often on sports topics, and is the author of two books of biographical profiles.

82-22801

45327

92
DOR　　 Biddle, Marcia
　　 McKenna

Tony Dorsett

X